The psychology of college success: a dynamic approach

The Psychology of College Success

A DYNAMIC APPROACH

HENRY CLAY LINDGREN
San Francisco State College

ROBERT E. KRIEGER PUBLISHING COMPANY
HUNTINGTON, NEW YORK
1980

Original Edition 1969
Reprint Edition 1980

Printed and Published by
ROBERT E. KRIEGER PUBLISHING COMPANY, INC.
645 NEW YORK AVENUE
HUNTINGTON, NEW YORK 11743

Library of Congress Cataloging in Publication Data

Lindgren, Henry Clay, 1914-
   The psychology of college success.

   Reprint of the edition published by Wiley, New York.
Includes index.
   1. College student orientation.   2. College students—
Psychology.   3. Academic achievement.   4. Study, Method
of.   5. Prediction of scholastic success.   I. Title.
[LB2343.3.L56 1980]   378'.198   79-25614
ISBN 0-89874-035-5

To C. GILBERT WRENN
for the many hours he spent
listening to the troubles of
a confused undergraduate

Preface

ALTHOUGH this is a book about success, it is impossible to discuss that attractive subject without considering failure as well. Indeed, one of the points I make in the book is that success comes through learning how to fail, and failures may, in a sense, be considered as way stations on the road to success.

Not all students learn from failure, however. If past experience is any indication, more than half of the two million students who are starting college this year will drop out and will not complete the two-, three-, or four-year course they have started.

This prediction is all the more disturbing, since the great majority of those who will drop out have the capacity to succeed. As a citizen of the world, I am appalled at the wastage this loss of talent represents, for we are far short of having enough trained and educated people to provide essential services and to do the jobs that need doing. As a teacher and a counselor I am moved to sympathy by the frustration, discouragement, and psychic pain that most of these students will experience before they find out that, for one reason or another, they must leave college.

I am also in sympathy with a group of "partial failures"—those who *do* complete their courses but whose success in their chosen field will be something less than would be expected. These students will not fail, in the conventional sense, but their disappointments at not performing up to their expected standards will nonetheless be real and often poignant.

In addition to my sympathy for these educational casualties I also feel depressed when I realize that most of this could have been prevented if remedial measures had been taken at the right time. We have plenty of data to show that the majority of students who are not doing very well or who even are at the very brink of failure can make dramatic recoveries if they participate in almost any type of organized help: tutoring, how-to-study courses, group therapy, counseling, reading clinics, and the like.

As we dig into the background of these failures and disappointments, we routinely run into two major causes: one that is attitudinal or emotional in nature, and the other, a matter of deficiency in one or more skills. These two types of shortcomings are generally interrelated. Students who have verbal problems—that is, students who cannot read rapidly and with comprehension and who cannot express themselves adequately in speech and writing when dealing with moderately complex material—are almost always individuals who, in the past, have not been particularly interested in developing such skills. Many of them, indeed, have felt quite negative about the insistence of high school English teachers that they read more books and improve their writing. Their attitudes and their deficiencies reinforce each other. Because of their apathy or their resistance, they did not learn the skills they now need, and because they had not learned the skills, they felt and also now feel negative toward them. I mention this particular interlocking set of attitudes and skills because it is a crucial one where college success is concerned—even practical junior college courses like floriculture, drafting, and practical nursing call for the use of communication skills. Attitudes toward getting involved academically and the ability to use study techniques are another pair of motives and skills that have a very important relationship to college success or failure, and there are still others.

The breakdown point at which students experience failure or disappointment comes when their skills fall short of instructor demands; hence the emphasis in most how-to-study books and courses is on the development of the necessary skills. My experience, however, leads me to believe that attitudes should have a higher priority than they ordinarily receive. In my opinion, when how-to-study measures succeed, they do so because students have developed the supporting and reinforcing motives that are needed before they can bring themselves to acquire and practice these skills. Indeed, those students who have the drive and the dedication to succeed often develop the needed skills and techniques on their own without any outside help. This is shown by the relatively large numbers of "overachievers" who graduate each year, some of them with honors. These are students who have dedicated and committed themselves to the tasks of learning, but whose aptitudes, as measured by psychological tests, would have led one to expect failure of them, or, at best, only modest success.

Attitudes, in my opinion, are paramount. I say this partly because my professional biases lead me to trust human beings more than techniques, and attitudes, being largely emotional in character, are closer to the unique and human elements within us than are techniques. My appraisal is also based on more than thirty years of successes and failures in working with thousands of willing and unwilling learners of all ages, ranging from nursery schoolers to candidates for graduate degrees, adult education students, servicemen, and applicants for rehabilitation. During these years I have played many roles: teacher, counselor, adviser, therapist, and researcher. I have continued to work in this difficult and complex field because I am interested in learning and am fascinated by the problems, difficulties, and challenges it poses.

My conclusion regarding the importance of attitudes in success or failure in learning is drawn not only from countless hours of talking with students about their learning problems but from my own learning experiences as well. Time and time again, in my encounters with students, I have been struck by the fact that everyone seems to want to acquire better *techniques* of learning but is uninterested in or even resistive to the need to experience the kind of attitudinal or emotional changes that must precede or accompany any effort at learning if it is to succeed. The reasons for this reluctance are fascinating, and we shall examine them from time to time in this book. In fact, it was partly my interest in the emotional factors in learning that led me to write it.

And now we come to the main purpose of the book: it was written in the hope that the student who reads it will gain some new and useful perspectives on learning and its problems, perspectives that will enable him to make a fresh start toward the successful completion of his college career.

As you go through the book, you will encounter a number of study techniques, some of which have been described in detail. I have, however, tried to keep these to the minimum. There are some excellent manuals specializing in study techniques that may be found in any college bookstore or library, and this book is not intended to supplant them, but rather to provide an antidote to what I consider to be one of their major failings. Whenever you are ready to make a real commitment to the tasks of learning, however, you would do well to read two or three of these manuals and to use whatever suits your special needs. If this book gets you as far as reading one of these manuals or, better yet, developing some of your own study techniques, it will have begun to succeed.

You will also find some advice in this book. I feel apologetic about this, for I know that if there is one thing that students have too much of, it is advice. Most of the advice they get is, furthermore, both unnecessary and irrelevant. But there are two problems that an author of a book like this faces. One is the difficulty of talking about learning and its problems without throwing out an occasional suggestion; the other is the need to provide something for students to start with—a kind of pump primer, so to speak. Although the advice I have included may be unnecessary, I feel reasonably sure that it is relevant.

Much of what I have said in this book has controversial overtones. I have already opened up one major controversy—that is, my affirmation that attitudes are basic to techniques, as far as learning is concerned. This controversy alone is worth several lively discussions, and I shall consider the book unsuccessful if it fails to stir up such debates. It does not matter whether I win the debate: one of my major objectives is to get you to think about learning and to raise questions about the way it should be done. When it comes to learning, most people are prisoners of a kind of "conventional wisdom," as John Kenneth Galbraith would put it, and it is only by questioning it that progress can be made. After all, conventional wisdom has not been of much help to the millions of college students who fail each year. Perhaps what they need is a fresh viewpoint, and that is what is attempted here. In any event, controversy leads to discussions, and it is my devout hope that this book will provide enough controversial material to serve as the basis of many discussions among students.

I cannot, however, take full credit for the ideas in this book, controversial or otherwise. They have, all of them, been borrowed or stolen from colleagues and students too numerous to mention and most of them long forgotten. Only the setting I have given them is original. Nevertheless, I would like to mention the helpful suggestions and encouraging support received from Eugene Raxten of Los Angeles Valley College. Finally, I am particularly grateful for the assistance given me by Edythe Moore, who typed the manuscript and served as a one-person reaction panel for the ideas expressed.

Henry Clay Lindgren

December 1968

Contents

The psychology of college success: a dynamic approach

CHAPTER ONE

College and you

WHAT kinds of goals do most college students have?

WHAT kind of student is likely to have doubts about staying in college?

WHAT do extrinsic and intrinsic motives have to do with success in college?

WHY should students conceal their motives even from themselves?

WHAT do defense mechanisms have to do with college success or failure?

THE meaning of *success*: Why is it important?

EVERYONE knows that college students have more freedom than high school students, but freedom for *what*?

WHAT important decision must every college student make?

COLLEGE is likely to be more stressful than high school: What effect does this have on students?

WHAT answers do colleges provide for students' problems?

"... and then the prof said: 'The next paper will be due Monday.' You know, in three years of high school I don't think I wrote even *four* papers, and now these guys want a paper a week. I tell you, I'm about to climb up the wall with all this writing!"

"I didn't get bad grades in high school—mostly C's and some B's. I admit I didn't work very hard—more interested in having a good time. But now I'm working my head off and I'm failing. What goes on here, anyway?"

"I read my notes after the physics lecture and they were a mess of nothing. I couldn't make head nor tail out of them. So I just memorized the terms and the formulas. I'll do well to get a D in the course."

"I'm so confused that I don't know *which* way to turn. High school wasn't like this. Sure, I had my problems, but I *liked* high school. I wish I was back there; I'd go see Miss Kubrick and she'd help me work it out. Miss Kubrick was a real person, but these people look right through you as if you weren't there."

"College is OK, I guess. But my brother down at the plant is doing OK, too. With overtime and night differential, he's really raking it in. So I ask, what does college get me that my brother hasn't got? College is supposed to help you get ahead, but sometimes I think I'm losing ground."

Unhappy, perplexed, frustrated, lost, depressed, disappointed, irritated, confused. These terms describe the feelings that come over almost every college student at times, particularly during the first few months, when he feels the full impact of the college experience. Although each student considers his experiences as unique, some feeling of disorientation and confusion is virtually universal. Even students who seem poised, happy, and in complete control of the situation have their moments of doubt and despair.

The reactions I have described are normal ones. They occur partly because the college experience is a new one, but there is more to it than that. They also occur because these students have entered an environment that, on the one hand, is probably as free as any-

2

thing they will ever experience but, on the other hand, is both demanding and exacting. The reasons for students' successes or disappointments in achievement may, for the most part, be found in the way in which the choices and the tensions are generated by this perplexing situation.

The decision to enter college, like many of the important moves you will make during your life, is a voluntary one. Students choose to enter college because it seems to be the best option out of a number of available possibilities. They make this choice because they see college as the best way of attaining certain goals of importance to them. This book is concerned with the success or failure of students to reach the goals they have set for themselves on entering college: why they find satisfaction or disappointment and what steps they may take to improve their chances for success and to avoid failure. To present as meaningful a picture as possible, we shall be concerned with ineffective behavior, with effective behavior, and with the feelings and attitudes that are, in the long run, probably more significantly than the kind of techniques students employ. As with most undertakings, motivation is a crucial factor, and we shall examine it again and again throughout this book.

Why go to college? It is characteristic of the human animal that everyone thinks his reasons for doing things are unique. There is probably some truth in this belief—certainly the exact pattern of motives is different for each of the six or seven million students who frequent the hundreds of college and university campuses across the nation. Nevertheless, some recurring themes appear in the lists of motives that any sample of students might give as explanations for their presence in college. Let us begin with some of these reasons.

There are many ways to classify or divide up the aims that students have when they enter college. We could, for example, classify them as "distant future" or "immediate future," or as "materialistic" or "idealistic." It may, indeed, be interesting for you to jot down some of your own motives. You may be surprised to see what they are, once you get them down on paper and start classifying them. Any classification system can aid in self-understanding

3

by suggesting clues to the motives behind the motives, but at this point we need classifications that are general—classifications that can be applied to any student's list of aims or motives and that will suggest something about the effectiveness or ineffectiveness of his behavior. Therefore, we shall discuss motivation in terms of the extent to which it is extrinsic or intrinsic—two dimensions that have considerable importance in terms of whether the college experience will be a successful one for you.

Extrinsic and intrinsic motives. Extrinsic motives, as the term indicates, have their sources *outside* of us and refer to behavior that we carry out in response to the demands and expectations of others, whereas intrinsic motives refer to behavior that is self-initiated. Here are some examples of extrinsic motivation:

Joe Blandon's family wants him to be a physician. He often says that he doesn't see much sense to the premed curriculum and that he is plodding along, taking courses as they come, because he knows that they must be completed before he can apply for admission to medical school. Sue Guft is not plodding, but drifting. She has not seriously thought of a major as yet, although she will be a junior next semester. She says that if her parents did not insist on her finishing college she would be an airline stewardess. Jack Kessel says that he is only going to school to keep out of the army. His brother, Sam, admits that the army may be a factor in *his* being in college, but says that he is more interested in the fact that college graduates make more money than high school graduates. Besides, employers expect a college degree these days. Joe Rosso has enrolled in the hotel-and-restaurant management course at the local community college. His family owns a motel and restaurant and expects him to take part in its management when he graduates two years from now. When asked why she is in college, Jill Shover answers with a question: "Where else is there to go? All my friends are here."

These motives are all extrinsic. It is as if the students were saying: "I have no real interest in what I am doing here. If others (medical school, parents, employers, friends) did not expect or de-

4

mand this of me, I would be doing something else." Their statements indicate that they they have a low degree of involvement in studying and learning and intend to commit no more of themselves than is required. Their stance toward college is passive rather than active.

Many students whose motivation is largely extrinsic do succeed in college, in the sense that they complete the requirements and graduate, although many more of them drop out and drift into something else. Whatever success they may have in college, however, comes at a higher psychological cost to them than it does for students whose motives are primarily intrinsic. The work we do to satisfy others is much more tedious and frustrating than the work we do in pursuit of our own motives. Our feelings of frustration may or may not be obvious but in any event, they will emerge in some form or other: deteriorating relations with family and friends, distractibility, restlessness and tension, depression, irritability, and even physical complaints (frequent colds, stomach upsets, and the like). That is what is meant by "higher psychological cost."

Students who attend college for reasons that are largely extrinsic are more likely to have doubts as to why they are in college than are other students. They are also more likely to be pessimistic about their chances for success. Although self-doubt can be a healthy condition at times, there is a tendency for it to be related to academic failure in its more extreme or chronic forms. One study of motivation found that entering students who feared failure in college were three times more likely to drop out than were students who did not report such fear. The same study showed that students who dropped out were also more likely to say that they were attending college to please their parents (Marks, 1967).

It comes as no surprise, of course, to find that students who drop out of college are more likely to mention extrinsic rather than intrinsic motives. Even under the best of conditions students are likely to encounter a great many frustrating and exasperating experiences, and those who are not intrinsically motivated—that is, those who are in college for reasons that are not important to them and who are not personally committed to getting an education—

5

have a more difficult time in forging ahead in spite of setbacks and obstacles. Carl Rogers (1961) points out that the only *real* learning is self-appropriated learning. No one can learn for you; learning is something you must do *by* yourself and for yourself. If the responsibility for your learning rests elsewhere, the chances are that whatever you learn will lack real significance for you. It will turn out to be a temporary acquisition, painfully memorized and quickly forgotten. This problem of acquisition and retention will be discussed in the next chapter, but here let me say that it is our intrinsic motives that determine what we will retain as a result of learning.

Concealed motives. We should not take what students say too literally, however. In the study just cited, even though the percentage of dropouts was higher among students who had anticipated failure, most of them actually did not drop out. Although their motivation was weaker than that of other students, it was much stronger than we would expect. Nor is it unusual to encounter students who describe their motivation as being shallow and extrinsic, yet who show every sign of benefitting from the college experience. Joe Blandon, the premed plodder we mentioned previously—the one whose family wants him to be a physician—is this type of person. Although he says that he is not interested in his courses and is only taking them because the medical school requires them, we notice that he is actually turning in an above-average performance in most of his courses and is even getting an occasional A. One explanation of this paradox, of course, is that the extrinsic reasons that Joe gives for being in college are not the whole story, but are instead a kind of cover or façade for motives that are personal and intrinsic in character. His general behavior in science courses suggests that he really finds them challenging and is investing more of himself than we would think from his offhand statement that he is only concerned about working off requirements and is pursuing a premed program merely to satisfy his family.

There are many reasons why people like Joe Blandon find it necessary to conceal their basically intrinsic motives with extrinsic ones. An obvious reason is this: an open admission that one finds

6

school work interesting and attractive may be embarrassing. To say that Joe enjoys doing course assignments may suggest to his friends that he has "sold out" or "gone over to the establishment"—that he has, in effect, taken on the values of the adult world and is in process of becoming one of "them." It is quite stylish these days to make much of the "generation gap"—the gulf that presumably separates youth from persons over 30 years of age, and some young people are ashamed to confess enthusiasm for activities that are also enjoyed by adults. Such a confession is considered by these students as being the equivalent of an admission of weakness or naiveté. According to their point of view, it is the task of the older generation to make demands and the responsibility of youth to resist them and to make counterdemands.

Although Joe may be concerned about the image he will present to his classmates, he is probably even more concerned about how he appears to himself. Is he the kind of person who is easily impressed by attempts of authority figures, like instructors, to get him involved in their fields of special interest? He would like to believe that he is not, that he is independent and free from such influence. In this respect he is not at all unusual; we all like to preserve an illusion of complete freedom in the face of compelling evidence that the kinds of decisions that we can actually make are somewhat restricted.

This does not mean that we are helpless prisoners of our fate or our environment, but simply that we are not free to make *all* decisions we think we can make. Joe is probably telling himself that he is *not* the kind of person who can be readily manipulated and molded by his elders, and his way of denying the effectiveness of their influence is to say to himself (and others) that he is *not* interested in the subject matter of the premed curriculum and is *only* doing whatever course work is required. By explaining his involvement in terms of the demands of some abstract, distant "other" (medical school requirements), he is able to shrug off any personal responsibility for his real commitment and interest. This does not, of course, keep him from turning certain extrinsic motives into intrinsic ones. Very likely his family's insistence that he become a

7

doctor has somehow become Joe's personal motive as well, although he might deny this by giving some excuse, such as "I'm going to complete premed and apply for med school, because nothing else seems to appeal to me." Such an explanation of his own behavior relieves him of the need to recognize that the decision is really his. It may also be regarded as a kind of insurance: if he fails, it is because of *their* plans, not his.

Defense mechanisms. Psychologists call this type of maneuver a *defense mechanism*. We all make use of such mechanisms in order to preserve our self-esteem, defend our beliefs, and avoid the chore of facing up to awkward facts about ourselves. Defense mechanisms actually serve a useful purpose in that they reduce anxiety and tension and thus enable us to go about the business of everyday living. If overused, they can interfere with normal functioning by concealing the true nature of our feelings from us or by keeping us from seeing realities that are obvious to everyone but ourselves.

Although defense mechanisms and how they operate is a fascinating topic, it is not my purpose to engage in an extended discussion of them here. I must point out, however, that they can lead us at times to make false conclusions, to resolve doubts that are best left unresolved, and they can keep us from getting to know and understand ourselves and our motives.

Attitudes toward success. Let me return to one item I mentioned in the discussion of Joe's use of defense mechanisms: the attitudes of his friends toward success, particularly toward success as defined by the adult world. Our attitudes toward success are of crucial importance in matters like survival in college and completion of a degree program, and these attitudes will depend, of course, on what success means to us. It is a good idea to stop at this point and jot down your reactions. What impressions does the word "success" make on you: Comfortable home with two children and a nice yard? An opportunity to serve others and help them to achieve a richer, fuller life? A walnut desk in a carpeted office, with your name on the door? A chance to be creative? What *does* success mean to you?

When most students list the meanings that success has for them, they tend to describe situations or goals located somewhere in the future. This occurs because college is usually perceived as a temporary phase, a preliminary stage before one becomes what he will *really* be—writer, teacher, wife and mother, computer programmer, or whatever. College may thus appear to be instrumental in aiding the attainment of a future goal or it may appear to be a kind of dreary ritual that one must walk through in order to attain the desired status. In either event, the student's feelings toward college are likely to be fairly passive and detached, and he thinks of himself sometimes as a bit of data to be processed, rather than as an active, involved participant. College work inevitably involves drudgery and frustration and, when the going becomes tedious, it is all too easy to reject the eventual goal as well as the rocky and difficult road that leads to it.

Some students today dismiss "success" completely as a goal not worth considering, taking their cue from certain writers of avant-garde literature. Success, according to these individuals, is essentially shallow and trivial, and they criticize those who are interested in success as driven, humorless, machinelike, or worse. Students who adopt this pose may be using it as a form of defense mechanism, one that serves to keep them from becoming involved in worthwhile, productive activity and at the same time protects them from the possible embarrassment of failure. Any kind of enterprise in which one invests something of himself carries a degree of psychological risk, and a student's decision that success is a goal that does not interest him gives him an excuse not to become involved.

The meaning of success. It can be argued, of course, that even those students who reject success as a goal are nevertheless, to some extent, interested in succeeding. Success for them may consist of maintaining the good will and acceptance of people like themselves, or it may mean "not succeeding in any *obvious* way," or even "failing dramatically." The point is that everyone has some set of personal goals, the attainment of which constitutes success of some sort.

The meaning that success has for us therefore takes on considerable importance. Unless we are able to develop some strong dedication and commitment to one or more long-range positive goals, we are likely to find ways of deciding that these goals are meaningless and not worth working for. Such a decision becomes doubly attractive and is an easy escape whenever the going becomes difficult. To avoid the commitment that long-range goals imply, we are tempted to focus on short-range goals for ourselves, thus ensuring the chance for success. Successful involvement in the college experience makes the most sense, however, when short-range goals are related to long-range goals. The solution to the problem is largely that of recognizing and enjoying the achievement of small steps in the direction of a long-range goal.

The rejection of long-range goals is made deceptively easy for us because they seem to represent options that are in the far future. We have no difficulty in deciding not to become a junior executive or an elementary school teacher as long as the choice does not appear to be an immediate one. This easy decision, however, misses the point. The decisions we make every day determine our future roles and the kinds of persons we will become. The person you are *becoming* today is the person you *will be* tomorrow. The choice of whether you are to succeed as a person is therefore one that faces you here and now.

This statement is relevant because every choice that a student must make is related directly or indirectly to his present status, to who he is. The choice to do or not to do an assignment for English 1A will depend, in part, on whether the student is ready to commit himself to his responsibilities on a here-and-now basis. It will also depend on whether he has attained enough maturity to involve himself in an intellectual undertaking. The question of maturity also arises with respect to his attitudes toward his instructor. Is he willing to accept the instructor as an aid, director, and pacemaker in an educational enterprise, or does he persist in attributing to him certain qualities and characteristics that are surprisingly like those he sees in his own father? Is his decision not to do the paper or not to turn it in on time related to his unwillingness to accept the fact that he lives in a world composed of other people and with whom he has a relationship characterized by mutual dependence? What he decides with respect to this single assignment in English 1A is not crucial, but the *way* in which he approaches such decisions *is* crucial. His progress through college will take place in terms of an infinite array of these decisions, some of them major, but most of them minor, and the approach he uses in resolving them will not only become a habitual pattern but will become part of him as well.

The same is true of grade school and high school, where progress also occurs as a result of making big and little decisions. College, however, is different in the sense that the decisions are much more your own. In high school, you were much more under the direct control and supervision of adults who were concerned—perhaps *too* concerned—that you would make a wrong move. There was some latitude for decision on your part, but the area of freedom was relatively restricted. College instructors are likely to be much less concerned, except in a very general way, with the decisions their students make. As a result, you are free to make your college experience an exciting intellectual adventure—something that high schools also hope for, incidentally, but are usually unable to let happen. In college, you can work what seems to you to be an exciting new idea into a term paper and enjoy a glow of appreciation when the instructor shares your enthusiasm. Original thinking is more likely to cause concern or even alarm in high schools. Instructors in college are more inclined to encourage students to do their own thinking, and there is a great deal more tendency to value ideas for their own sake. There are, of course, risks with respect to having ideas rejected, just as there is in high school, but college instructors differ in that they are *relatively* more tolerant. Much depends on how ideas are communicated. In fact, communication problems are so important that I shall devote an entire chapter to the subject.

The greater freedom to succeed, however, also implies a greater freedom to fail. The instructor may think the fine, exciting, original idea you put into your paper is not original at all, but banal, shallow, and "derivative." College instructors, as a rule, are much harder to please than high school teachers, and grades average a notch lower in college than they do in high school. Many a student finds that he is working harder and doing better work than he did in high school, but that he is earning lower grades.

The impact of the college experience. Perhaps the most obvious thing about college, as far as the newly arrived student is concerned, is that it is not like anything he has ever experienced before. He knew, of course, that it would be different, but it is different in ways that he did not anticipate. Perhaps he did not anticipate being lonely and isolated—an odd experience in the midst of hundreds of other people. He knows he belongs, yet he feels like an outsider. These feelings gradually diminish during the weeks after registration when friends are made and the campus begins to take on certain aspects of familiarity, but it returns from time to time, unexpectedly. The feeling of being alone and friendless may well up when the desk clerk at the reserved book desk says that all the books on the required reading list are out and will not be back until tomorrow morning at 8. They may reappear when the first paper in English comes back, marked "C+ for grammar and style, and D for content." It is at these times that one feels not only lost and alone, but exposed and vulnerable as well.

The very variety of experiences offered by colleges makes them different. One interacts with a wide assortment of students—young people from diverse backgrounds and representing a broad range of experiences and viewpoints. The fact that college is a free marketplace for ideas also contributes its share of confusion. There are, in addition, so many things to be aware of and to attend to that the effect may be one of continual distraction. The "input of stimuli," as the psychologists term it, is greater in college than in almost any other type of undertaking, and when new students try to cope with and sort out an overload of stimuli, confusion, anxiety, and frustration are certain to result. The combination will prove to be too much for some, and they will withdraw after a few weeks. For those who remain, however, learning to cope with the problems of an exciting and challenging new environment can yield some important rewards in terms of maturity, competence, and psychological growth.

12

Self-discovery and "becoming." What the college environment does to students is to change them. This is a recurring finding in dozens of studies that have been made of students before and after their college careers.[1] The college experience not only broadens their intellectual background and gives them more information and new skills, it changes their attitudes as well. It makes them more tolerant, more interested in intellectual activities, more curious, and more inclined to involve themselves in a wide variety of activities. These are all changes of maturity: they are characteristic of individuals who have become stronger and more competent as a result of their experience. What college has done for them is to give them a chance to *become,* to find new ways of self-affirmation. The college years are, for many students (probably the majority), years of self-discovery.

What I have been describing are the more significant outcomes of time spent at college. These are not outcomes that can be measured in terms of grade-point average or numbers of class hours completed. They show, instead, that a very significant kind of learning has taken place. They are indicators, so to speak, of the kind of personal success that comes through making choices, meeting challenges, and coping with the kinds of stresses and strains that are peculiar to the college environment.

Sources of influence and stimulation. College contributes through a number of channels to the intellectual, social and emotional growth I have been describing. The first and most obvious channel is the college classroom. The classroom experience can be boring, exciting, irritating, or reassuring, but it is, above all, a place where ideas are dispensed, traded, exposed, criticized, and analyzed. It is difficult to say how much of the gain in maturity that takes place in college can be attributed to classroom experiences. Perhaps very little is directly attributable, but it is safe to say that without the

[1] A recent study of 10,000 high school graduates discloses, for example, that those who entered college and continued on to graduation showed greater gains in personality development—growth in independence, intellectual interests, and enlightened self-awareness—than did those who did not attend. (Trent and Medsker, 1968).

13

confrontation with ideas that occurs in the classroom, the change would not have appeared.

The classroom is also a starting point for attempts at communication. If students played only passive roles in communication, and were only listeners and readers, probably little learning would take place. There are, however, many opportunities to participate actively. There are the quizzes, examinations, and assigned papers that give students opportunities for self-expression and for telling instructors (and themselves as well) what they have learned. In addition, there are countless opportunities to initiate informal conversations with fellow students, instructors, teaching assistants, departmental secretaries, and many other more or less interested people. Some of these conversations wax warm with controversy: so much the better. The more active and vital the involvement in such interaction, the more the exposure and the greater the opportunity for change and growth.

Much education takes place over the coffee cups in the college union and in the "bull sessions" in the residence halls. Some students find it easier to accept new ideas from other students than from their instructors. Expounding concepts and views to other students is another way in which learning takes place. When you discuss and explain an idea, it really becomes a part of you. Being able to participate in these conversations also gives you the feeling of intellectual competence, another plus value in favor of growth and maturity.

Trauma and triumph in learning. I have mentioned the stress and strains that students encounter as they progress through college. These more negative experiences also make their contribution. It is axiomatic that no significant learning ever takes place without some discomfort. First there is the embarrassment of feeling ignorant in the presence of so much knowledge. Then there is the discouragement that comes when one sees how much work has to be accomplished to attain even a small goal, like the completion of a mid-term report. There are also the frustrations and disappointments of occasional failure, as well as the feeling of emptiness that comes from an inability to achieve one's best capabilities. It is through

14

repeated attempts to deal with such problems that real learning and growth comes, and it takes struggles like these to achieve what Abraham Maslow (1962) called "peak experiences."

These peak experiences are not the only rewards that keep students going. While colleges create problems for students, they also provide some of the means for solving them. The antidote to the problem of loneliness is companionship, and the solution for confusion is the opportunity to talk out one's difficulties with students who share the same kinds of experience. Colleges also offer the freedom to experiment with off-beat ideas to see whether they have any value. Although these attempts usually end in failure, there is a degree of support and acceptance for such experiments that one does not find in other environments. The college environment is a structured environment: it operates according to schedules and there are certain tasks and roles that are expected of students and faculty. Within this more or less predictable framework, however, there is a great degree of flexibility. The structure may limit, but it also provides security and support. The flexibility and tolerance may be confusing and upsetting for the student who has never tasted freedom, but they do offer the chance to develop new identities. In short, there is something for everyone.

From the standpoint of psychological development, the college may be perceived as a *growth environment,* an environment in which individuals are expected to become more mature and in which conditions are arranged in such a way that growth actually takes place. It has, on the one hand, a *socializing* influence, in that students are helped to learn roles that will make them more effective adult members of society, and, on the other hand, a *stimulating* effect, in that students are exposed to new situations that require them to develop new perspectives and attitudes. As in other areas of life experience, the rewards and reinforcements accrue to those who are able to develop strength, maturity, and competence, whereas those who are inadequate are penalized, overlooked, and forgotten.

In other words, the goal of the college experience is essentially the goal of maturity. One can succeed only to the extent that one

15

becomes mature, while failure comes from an unwillingness to face the challenges and demands of the college environment, as well as from avoiding responsibilities and somehow missing or sidestepping opportunities to become more competent and more adequate.

CHAPTER TWO

Learning: a psychological process

WHAT does your concept of yourself have to do with what you learn and how you learn it?

How will college change you?

WHY have we forgotten so much of what we learned in high school?

WHY is it so difficult to memorize facts for a quiz?

MUST learning be painful?

WHAT is meant by reinforcement in learning?

Do mnemonic devices really help in memorizing?

How can we learn material that seems irrelevant and trivial?

WHAT can be learned from an instructor, other than information?

The college experience, as I pointed out in the opening chapter, is an opportunity to *become*. Becoming implies change, and change inevitably involves learning. The changes that take place in individuals who attend college consist of attitudes, values, reactions, and forms of behaving that have been *learned* by them. Those who have the most successful experiences in college are those who have taken advantage of opportunities to learn, whereas the least successful are those who either have found ways to avoid learning or who have been unequal to the learning tasks they have encountered.

There are essentially two major kinds of learning tasks that college students face: (1) the broader, long-range tasks that are related to the general topic of self-development we discussed in the opening chapter, and (2) the detailed, day-to-day tasks that are related to success in a particular subject or assignment. First, let us discuss the broader, long-range tasks.

Learning and the self-concept. We begin by presenting an idea that many psychologists interested in problems of human learning have found to be useful: that of self-concept (Combs and Snygg, 1959). The self-concept is, as term suggests, the concept we have of ourselves. It may be said to lie (Figure 1) at the very center of our world. It is the self we think we are, as differentiated from the world around us, or "not-self." Part of the not-self consists of people, beliefs, and other kinds of objects and events in which we find ourselves involved and with which we identify to a greater or lesser degree. The farther away from the self-concept objects, or events, or other people are located in this diagram, the less we are involved in them and the less our feelings of concern.

During infancy and childhood some important changes take place in the relationship between our self-concept and the other areas represented in Figure 1. For one thing, the entire area expands as we become more aware of ourselves and the world around us. For another, the boundaries between areas change in accordance with ·alterations in the way we view ourselves and our environment. As we emerge from childhood, we become less emotionally attached to certain objects in our immediate environment, like toys and articles of clothing, but we also develop a deeper psychological

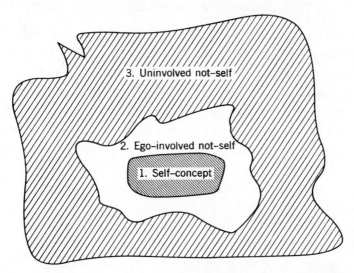

Figure 1. Our personal world or self-structure. *Key*: (1) *Self-concept or ego.* Who we are, or think we are. (2) *Ego-involved not-self.* Our area of involvement; the objects, events, people, beliefs, concepts, and values that are of interest to us, in which we are involved, and in which we have some degree of emotional investment. (3) *Uninvolved not-self.* The rest of the world, of which we are aware but in which we have only passing involvement.

involvement in certain people (friends, certain social groups and organizations, and loved ones) as well as in mankind as a whole.

Although changes in the relationship between the self-concept and our environment continue throughout the life span, they take place at a rapid and sometimes confusing pace during the college years. Specific concepts that during adolescence seemed firmly fixed in the ego-involved region move toward the uninvolved area as we become more objective and more interested in ideas in general. As we are exposed to new models, our concepts of ourselves change, and ideas we never heard of previously become attractive, find a place within the ego-involved area, and even merge into the self-concept. Although college changes us in ways that are apparent to all who know us, probably the most significant changes occur in the less visible areas of the self, in our view of ourself as a person in relation to the world in which we live.

The learning of sense and nonsense. These changes take place, as I have said, through learning. This does not mean that we absorb everything that comes our way, in an uncritical fashion. On the contrary, we learn only those things that make some kind of sense to us. The whole world of our awareness, ourselves included, takes on meaning only in terms of what its objects and events *mean to us*. The entire self-structure represented by Figure 1 has meaning only with respect to its center—that is, in terms of its orientation to the self-concept. Information that has no particular meaning may be acquired and given temporary status in the uninvolved not-self area for some special occasion, like the need to pass a test, but is "dropped out of the field" and forgotten as soon as it is no longer required. Virtually all college students learned to multiply and divide fractions when they were in grade school, but most of them have forgotten these skills by the time they enter college. The same is true of at least nine tenths of the factual material learned in high school. The only data that we retain within the boundaries of our self-structure are those that somehow possess interest and value for us. The rest is treated as nonsense and is dropped when the need to take examinations has passed and the courses are over.

Not only is it difficult to retain material that makes no sense to us, but it is also difficult to acquire it, even on a temporary basis. Data that have no meaning for us cannot be oriented to the self, and we keep rejecting them as foreign bodies that do not belong within the self-structure. The fact that we must acquire them temporarily in order to pass an examination makes them important for our welfare but does not give them real meaning. We must therefore work much harder to learn irrelevant data, to force them into some place within the personal world. As long as we attempt to acquire information that has no personal relevance, we must work long and hard for relatively meager results. One solution is that of finding more efficient ways of learning irrelevant information. This is, of course, the short-range approach. The more effective method is that of seeking or permitting the kind of changes within the self-structure that would give the material to be learned more relevance and hence more meaning.

Learning and the area of self-involvement. It is a fact of life that some people possess more information than others. Let us call these more informed people "educated," recognizing that education may be acquired independently as well as through participation in the college experience. Educated people differ from persons of lesser attainment because they have more information, are familiar with more concepts, and have mastered a larger number of skills. There are other differences as well, but we shall focus our attention briefly on differences in retention. If what is learned and retained depends on the extent to which it makes sense to the learner, then it follows that people who are more interested and involved in the world around them will make better learners than those who are less involved. In other words, educated people learn more effectively than less educated people. Education is not only the result of learning, it also facilitates further learning.

Students who make the most successful learners usually are more complex than most people because they have more interests and are more broadly and deeply involved in the world around them. What happens to these people as they proceed through the college experience is that they become even more complex, develop still more interests, and become involved in still more activities. Area 2 in Figure 1 is an ever-expanding one for them. The fact that college produces this kind of change sheds some light on the reasons why some students experience a great many problems in learning and retention: these individuals are likely to be the ones whose interests are more restricted and who are involved in a limited range of activities. The boundaries of Area 2 in Figure 1 are, for them, fixed, rigid, and stationary. Such students suffer from a chronic inability to relate material to be learned to other aspects of their lives: there are just not enough facets to relate things to. Perhaps schools are to be criticized because the subject matter they teach is not relevant to the lives of students, but it is also fair to say that students who have the broadest interests also have the least difficulty in retaining what schools have to teach.

This brings us back to another topic we discussed in Chapter 1: motivation. The more interested and excited students are about broadening their horizons, the more success they will have in learning and retaining what they learn.

We should observe, however, that there is a natural reluctance on the part of students to develop the kind of interests that lead to involvement in the processes of real learning—that is, learning for retention. This reluctance is often attributed to laziness—perhaps unfairly—because many students work hard at memorizing material for their recitations and examinations and still have difficulties with retention. The problem, instead, seems to run deeper. As I pointed out in Chapter 1, changes are always accompanied by some discomfort, no matter how welcome they may be, and the kind of learning that is the most significant results in a considerable degree of discomfort. Significant learning will result in some changes in the student's self-concept, some alteration in the border area that lies between the self and the not-self. These adjustments are generally accompanied by some degree of tension and even of pain. Hence the kind of learning that leads to retention may be shunned because it leads to what the student considers would be more changes than he is prepared to make in his self-concept or in his relationship to the world of his awareness.

I have previously mentioned the problem of reluctance to change, and I shall touch on it again because I believe that (1) it is fundamental to success or failure in college and that (2) students will be able to cope more effectively if they know what the problem is. As I shall point out in the next chapter, knowing what a problem is enables us to plan strategies that can be used to solve it. It also enables us to ask questions and find answers. No one is more helpless than the person who is troubled and frustrated but who does not know why.

Learning as reinforcement. Now let us shift our attention from the broad and general to the specific and detailed. Learning may, as I have said, be perceived as a process of growth and personal development; it also may be perceived as a process whereby the responses that we make to our environment are either strengthened because they are rewarded or reinforced or are weakened or extinguished because they do not get this positive treatment. Many psychologists believe that this view of learning sufficiently explains the appearance and persistence of all forms of learned behavior, from nervous habits like hair twisting and ear pulling to complex behavior like cigarette smoking and getting along with college instructors.

The key process in this formulation is *reinforcement*. A response (which may consist, for example, of producing a fact on demand) is learned and may be repeated because it has been reinforced. If it is not reinforced, it will not be learned. To apply this formulation to the successful students we mentioned previously, we can say that they are able to muster more facts and techniques in dealing with situations because such responses were reinforced for them, but not for others. The student who learns facts, but who forgets them, presumably does so because they were not adequately reinforced or are no longer reinforced.

It is fair to say that psychologists who favor the self-concept approach to learning have many faults to find with the reinforcement approach. I discuss reinforcement here, however, because it does have some direct applications to the kinds of problems encountered by students.

Research with reinforcement shows that it has the most effect if it follows closely upon the heels of the response that is to be learned. One of the problems with much of the learning activity that takes place in college is that reinforcement may be delayed for weeks and months. A student may not be held accountable for the material he reads during the first week of the semester until a midterm examination six weeks later, and even then he may not get the results of the examination until another two weeks have gone by. Whatever reinforcement he gets may also be highly selective. Since a given examination can cover only a small percentage of what has been presented in the course, very few of the potential responses the student can make ever get reinforced at all.

There are, however, a number of ways that students can organize their work so that their efforts at learning can have a better chance to be reinforced. The student who begins his reading assignment by jotting down questions he expects will be answered and who goes back to them when he has finished reading is likely to experience some reinforcement. In this instance, the reinforcement comes through satisfaction in being able to answer the questions. Students who study in pairs and who query each other on the material they have read may also experience reinforcement. Students' attitudes toward a course or an academic field may change because they make the acquaintance of someone majoring in that area. Such an acquaintanceship may reinforce attitudes that are favorable to success in that field. It is easier to be interested in a field when your friends are interested in it as well. Interests and attitudes may be reinforced as well as informational responses.

Memorization. This topic is included here because a certain amount of memorization is necessary for some subjects and because some of the techniques that contribute to the efficiency of memorization also aid in other types of study activity.

As my earlier discussion of learning, retention, and the self-system suggests, the major problem in memorizing is that of meaning. If material is meaningful, we do not have to work so hard in finding a place for it within the self-system. The problem often occurs, however, that material must be learned before we have developed the necessary supporting and reinforcing interests, values, perspectives, and concepts. The whole process of education moves slowly, and it is often necessary to press forward in some areas before we are psychologically ready to do so. Therefore, some memorization is unavoidable, and the problem is that of doing it as efficiently as possible.

Sometimes meaning can be introduced artificially by what is termed a *mnemonic device* or a *memory crutch*. The rhyme that begins "Thirty days hath September, . . ." is an example of a device we use to remind ourselves which months have thirty days and which have thirty-one. The order in which colors appear in the spectrum may also be remembered by the name "Roy G. Biv" (for red, orange, yellow, green, blue, indigo, and violet). These "crutches" may be very helpful in memorizing key material, and the invention of such devices may make learning tasks more interesting. However, crutches work best when we are able to use them in connection with an overall conceptual framework that enables us to organize the information we need to remember.

24

Another problem in memorizing involves the relative desirability of committing to memory larger or smaller amounts of a body of interrelated material. Should we memorize poems one line at a time, or should we attempt the entire poem? The research favors the larger rather than the smaller morsel. There are individual differences, of course. Some people evidently have more difficulty in memorizing larger passages, perhaps because they lose the thread of meaning if the block of material they try to commit to memory is too extensive. What is a part for one person is a whole for another. The problem is basically one of meaning: if the body of material is too extensive, it is likely to be confusing and to lack meaning. If, on the other hand, one commits to memory a number of segments of material, there is the danger of forgetting how they are interconnected. Unless we can see how they fit together in some kind of sense-making framework, we must expend a great deal of time and energy in frequent review.

Review is a necessary activity in any kind of learning. It is best accomplished if it is functional—that is, if it can be done in connection with a useful activity. The physics major has little difficulty in remembering mathematical processes, because he uses them frequently. Students majoring in art history also are able to remember the terms that make up the specialized vocabulary they learned in their introductory courses because they use it every day in communicating with one another and with their professors about their work. The more that material we have learned becomes a part of or is related to our everyday activity, the more frequently we review it and the less difficulty we have in remembering it.

Where we experience the chief difficulty, of course, is in memorizing material that is *unrelated* to everyday activities. The English major enrolls in geology because the college requires him to take a science course as a prerequisite for graduation. He therefore finds that he must learn about synclines, anticlines, faults, and igneous intrusions—terms that seem to have nothing to do with the life he lives, the things he does, his hopes and expectations—that is, with *any* dimension of Figure 1. The simplest thing to do, it seems, is to commit everything to memory, by rote drill, pass the necessary examinations, and forget it for all time. However, this is not the simplest but rather the more difficult approach. A simpler approach would be to try to see the world around him as a geologist does—in terms of folded and faulted strata; igneous, metamorphosed, or sedimentary rock; or whatever. If the student were able to adopt these perspectives, geology and its special vocabulary would make more sense to him and his learning tasks would take less time and energy. He would still have to do some memorizing, but at least whatever he was trying to learn would make some sense with respect to the world he perceives. He would be able to work with larger rather than smaller concepts, because he would be able to see interrelationships more readily.

Since our English major's chief interests lie in the field of literature and communication, he is not going to be as involved in dealing with geological concepts as would a student of mining engineering. Consequently he would probably have to spend more time with the mechanical aspects of memorization. For example, he would have to be sure that he reviewed the necessary terminology at frequent intervals. In doing this he should confine his review to brief periods. The periods should be long enough for him to get a feeling for the material and have some success in recall, but they should not be so long that he would get oversaturated and bored with the details. Each person must discover for himself how long a review period or any kind of a study period should be. This is one reason why some kind of scheduling is needed for effective studying. Generally, however, the more efficient approach is that of interspersing periods of work on subjects that seem less relevant and interesting with periods spent on subjects that seem more relevant and interesting. All material has some degree of potential interest, and the student's work is facilitated if he can find something of interest in everything: these are the keys to efficient and effective study. We would be something less than realistic if we insisted that everything be equally interesting to everybody. Since we all have studies we enjoy more and those that we enjoy less, we must work out some kind of arrangement whereby we spend an adequate amount of time on the subjects that are less attractive and in which we feel less involved.

In other words, we have more of a problem in learning material from less preferred courses, partly because this material seems to be less relevant to our self-concepts and partly because we do not find learning experiences as readily reinforced. Our English major is likely to find more reinforcement in doing an adequate job of literary criticism for a favorite English professor than in learning the sequence of geological periods. He feels a greater degree of identity with his English professor than with his geology professor, and the favorable opinion of the former is worth more to him, psychologically speaking, than is the favorable opinion of the latter. He sees himself, furthermore, as becoming a specialist in English rather than in geology, and progress toward the former goal has more psychological value for him than progress toward the latter goal.

There are, however, a number of things he can do to compensate for his tendencies to work on English assignments and to avoid geology assignments. The more aware he is of this tendency, the better able he is to do something about it. He can, for example, plan his study periods so that geology gets its due before he turns his attention to English. Or he can find ways, as I have suggested, to make geology more interesting, relevant, and meaningful. He can also develop a broader image of what an educated man should be. If he can see that an educated man should have an understanding of the physical world, as well as of the world of literature, he will be in a better position to accept the need to become involved in activities that will contribute to this larger view.

The basic problem, as I have pointed out, is that of motivation. The process of identifying new goals inevitably brings about changes in our self-concept. These changes lead to involvement in new activities. Experiences we had rejected now become potentially reinforcing, and we find new ways to be reinforced and rewarded.

Learning from models. A great deal of learning is imitative. This is particularly true of the learning of attitudes and values—

aspects of the personality that are fundamental to the desire to learn. It is quite likely that many of the changes that take place in a student as a result of four years of college are the result of coming in contact with a wide range of individuals who represent modes of thinking and feeling that are different from those he has experienced up to that point. Some of these individuals attract and interest him, and their behavior and ways of thinking become patterns, so to speak, which he uses as models for his own behavior. Some psychologists believe that a great deal of learning in social situations (such as that which occurs in a classroom, for example) takes place through our tendency to imitate the behavior of models.

The models that college students encounter and that may have a significant effect on their motivation, as well as on what is learned and how it is learned, consist of both instructors and other students. We shall examine these two types of models and their effects on learning in Chapters 5 and 6.

CHAPTER THREE

Learning: a problem-solving approach

WHY is it that in some courses you do everything that is required, but have little to show for it when the term is over?

How do the learning strategies of successful and unsuccessful students differ?

IN what way are the strategies you use effective? In what way are they ineffective?

How can you learn by *not* focusing on learning?

IN what ways can a problem-solving approach help in a course like English literature in which there are no assigned problems?

How can students cope with required courses in which they have no interest and which are poorly taught?

WHY should you overanticipate deadlines?

How "flexible" should study schedules be?

GETTING an education: Is it a game?

WHAT kind of people stay in college and complete their work? What kind drop out? What is it that makes a dropout drop?

The place of strategy in learning. In this chapter I shall describe an approach to learning that a great many students have used successfully not only in completing course requirements but also in deriving benefits from their college experience that otherwise they would have missed. The word I shall use in discussing this approach is *strategy*. Indeed, I might say that a major difference between successful and unsuccessful students lies in the kind of strategies they employ.

The term *strategy,* as used with respect to learning, refers to any sequence of decisions purposefully undertaken to attain a goal (Bruner, Goodnow, and Austin, 1956). Hence it refers both to the planning that serves as a basis for working toward long-range goals and to the kinds of methods that students use consistently in their approach to college work. Some strategies are obviously more successful than others. Strategies that lead a student to become sensitive to the issues, concepts, and procedures that are deemed important by experts in a field are likely to lead in the long run to academic success, whereas strategies that are aimed at keeping instructor demands at a minimum and in blocking their effectiveness may succeed only in terms of short-range goals. However, these goals are less likely to be consistent with success as it is usually viewed. Actually, strategy aimed at short-range goals, and which is concerned with maintaining the highest possible degree of psychological comfort, may fail in the end. The student who employs this strategy is likely to adopt a passive attitude with respect to his instructors, waiting until they make a demand before he makes a response. The student who has devised effective strategies, on the other hand, will be better able to anticipate instructor demands and will, in fact, take the initiative to prepare himself to meet all kinds of challenges and to carry out a wide variety of activities in the field. The student whose strategy is essentially passive is vulnerable in another way: instructional demands that are in any way unusual are likely to throw him into a state of confusion or even panic.

Learning and self-involvement. Learning, as I pointed out in the opening chapter, is *becoming*—growth, self-development, and self-enrichment. It is both a process and an outcome that actually occur as by-products of other activities, particularly those activities that enable us to encounter new concepts and ideas and to perceive ourselves and the world in new ways. Learning may also occur spontaneously, as the result of chance experiences. It may take place as a result of sitting through a lecture or reading a book, although there is no guarantee that such activity will lead to learning. We have all had courses in which we did everything that was required of us and yet, in retrospect, we must admit that we obtained little, if anything, to show for the time and energy expended.

Certain experiences are more likely than others to result in learning and growth. Generally, the more we involve ourselves in a situation, the more we learn. Notice that the approach here is one of self-involvement, not of memorization. When we memorize, we are saying, in effect, "The only thing that counts is to acquire this information." There is no hint of any desire to change, to accommodate ourselves, to develop new perspectives. We see what is to be learned as foreign, as if it were *outside* ourselves, and we are going to possess it (perhaps temporarily) for some particular purpose, such as that of passing an examination or quiz. This does not mean that memorization has no place in the educational process, but it does mean that the function of memorization is a restricted one, one that is concerned with aspects of behavior that may *seem* like learning but actually are not.

Learning, as I have said, is a by-product of activities in which we are involved and committed. Because of this involvement and commitment, we see things differently, develop new skills and attitudes, and are changed by the process in a number of ways. We have learned by *not* focusing on learning as such: it came as an incidental result of our efforts and activities.

Strategies facilitate learning when they enable us to find ways to involve ourselves. The decision to plan a strategy is actually a first step in committing ourselves. Thinking about strategies gets us into the mood to learn. A task or series of tasks that until the present had seemed alien, forbidding, boring, and trivial now takes on new aspects. What had seemed to be impossible now seems to be possible, because a basic assumption to the planning of strategies to tackle *any* kind of problem is that the problem can be solved.

As we plan our strategies, we become alert to possibilities that otherwise would not have occurred to us. We become more aware of our own aims as we outline the objectives of the course for which we are planning strategies. Our awareness of these goals enables us to raise questions with ourselves about the progress we are making in the course, and also facilitates carrying out our strategies.

A question could be raised, of course, as to whether strategies are necessary. Probably few learners deliberately plan strategies in connection with the courses they are taking. However, all successful learners do use strategies to some degree whether they are aware of it or not. The strategies they use are likely to be the ones they have developed and learned to use in courses taken previously. Elliot Vandercamp tries to read all the textbooks assigned in his classes within the first week of the term. He does not, to be sure, read them intensively—he only "skims" them. He says that this practice gives him a general idea of what is going on in his courses. Sally Stoltz types all her papers, whether typed papers are required or not. She says that typing a paper enables her to organize it better and to see mistakes in grammar and punctuation. Sally's approach actually requires her to do a paper twice—once in rough draft and once in finished form, but she believes that the revised version is enough of an improvement to be worth the effort.

The reason why Elliot and Sally are successful students is not so much because they have used this or that technique but because they have a general approach that produces results. The two techniques mentioned merely reflect the kind of overall strategy these two students use, although neither is aware of using what we are calling a "strategy." The major difference between the strategies used by Elliot and Sally and those used by a less successful student is that *their* strategies produce results, attuned as they are to the general goals of self-development and growth. The less successful student has a strategy, too, although he is no more aware of using it than Elliot and Sally are of using theirs. His strategy is more likely to be self-defeating. Let us take a look at a less successful strategy.

Clyde Opel maintains that one should take advantage of the social as well as the intellectual aspects of college. In this he is no different from Elliot and Sally, who also believe that social activities are important. Clyde, however, mentions this concern so often that we are led to wonder whether he is trying very hard to convince himself of something. When we observe his behavior, it seems as though he has given social goals a higher priority than the intellectual ones. His statements thus suggest that he is trying to reassure himself that this priority is appropriate. There are many ways in which Clyde's general strategy reveals itself. Early in the term he takes steps to find out how insistent his instructors are with respect to attendance and assignments. If they are, as he terms it, "rigid," then he resigns himself to doing what is required. He postpones doing required reading until the day before an examination. As he says, "I work better under pressure." After an examination, he may complain bitterly to other students about questions being unfair, but he says nothing to the instructor. In fact, Clyde has never said anything to an instructor except a "Hello" when he happens to meet one in the hall or some other spot where confrontation is unavoidable. It is difficult to determine why Clyde uses the strategy he does. He is not involved in campus politics and is a member of no social groups. He spends the time he saves by cutting classes, where attendance is not required, in the college union talking with anyone who will listen. He watches more television than most students, and participates only haphazardly in intramural sports.

It is clear, even from this brief description, that Clyde's strategy is both passive and negative. Somehow it seems calculated to keep him from being involved in anything. He may, indeed, have a fear of self-commitment. Every so often his strategy fails, and he finds himself involved and interested in spite of himself. In general, however, he tries to avoid courses in which this is likely to happen, because he has difficulty in resisting the demands of instructors when he is interested in a course. He would have more to show

33

for his time if he could overcome the personal problems that prevent his developing self-commitment and involvement. If he were able to do this, he could then begin to develop strategies that would be more productive, as far as learning and growth are concerned.

THE PROBLEM-SOLVING APPROACH

The strategy I shall discuss is based on the assumption that the attainment of any goal or objective may be perceived as a problem to be solved. I do not refer here to the kind of problem that appears in mathematics textbooks or in laboratory manuals, since these are problems in which all the facts specified are relevant—that is, problems in which every bit of data is related to the solution. The problems of getting an education are, like the problems of everyday living, quite different from textbook problems because they are made up of a shifting, changing array of objects and events—people, attitudes, conditions, feelings, regulations, resources, and the like. Some of these data are obviously relevant to the solution of the problem, but many are not. At almost every step in solving educational problems we are faced with the need to determine which aspects of our situation are relevant and which are irrelevant. Sometimes it even helps to sit down with pencil and paper and make a list in order to sort them out properly.

However, before one can decide which variables or aspects in our situation are relevant and important, it is essential to know what the problem is. The problem, in other words, must be known and, if possible, described. Of course, problems, in themselves, have no "reality"—they are merely ways of analyzing, organizing, and describing situations and possible eventualities. Inasmuch as problems have no "reality" as such and exist only in terms of our perceptions, we can use any approach we wish in identifying them and describing them. We are not completely free of reality, however, because the decisions we make are going to be tested out

34

in the real world, and if we distort or overlook important consid-
erations, we can fail. The problem-solving approach therefore has
a degree of risk to it, and many people are unwilling to use it
for that reason, preferring to "play it by ear" and to take things as
they come. This course of action is familiar and seems (superficially,
at least) to be risk-free. Actually, nothing is risk-free, and the problem-solving approach may be "safest" in the long run because it
enables the problem-solver to take more possibilities into account
and thus become more aware of reality.

What is the problem? The first step, as I have said, is to determine what the problem is. One way to identify the problem in a
given course—say, English Literature—is to begin by making a
list of all the problems that might be related to the course. Let us
assume that Clyde Opel experienced a small disaster last term: he
underestimated the "rigidity" of an instructor and failed a course.
As a result, his average has dropped to a precarious level. One
more failure and he may be placed on probation and perhaps even
disqualified. He has had a bad scare and must revise his strategy
in order to insure his survival in college. Clyde's list of problems
might begin with the item: "How to get at least a B in English
Literature." This is, of course, related to a number of other problems, such as "How to stay in college and get a degree" and "How
to avoid spending so much time on English literature that I jeopar-
dize my chances for passing grades in other classes." It is clear
that Clyde's motivation is intrinsic in the sense that he is concerned about his own survival in college, but it is extrinsic in the
sense that he views his survival in terms of what he must do in
order to satisfy the demands of other people.

Inasmuch as Clyde is not likely to use a bona fide problem-
solving approach in dealing with the situation that confronts him,
let us examine the situation faced by Elliot Vandercamp who is
also taking English literature. Elliot is a physics major; he does not
particularly care for literature courses and probably would not take
one if the college had not required that all students, irrespective of
their majors, take a certain number of humanities courses. Since
he has to take a humanities course, whether he wants to or not,

Elliot decides that he might as well get some personal return out of the time he must invest. Furthermore, Elliot is a rather methodical person, and using a problem-solving approach is almost second nature with him; hence he sits down to see what kind of problems the course presents. He decides that his main problem may be stated as "Deriving some personal benefit from a course in English literature."

This problem is related to Elliot's attitudes toward literature in general. Like many science majors, he found high school English classes rather uninteresting, and he is not very optimistic about this particular course. Nevertheless, he is determined to get something of value out of the courses he must take outside his major field of interest. This decision, to be sure, was somewhat reinforced by Elliot's major adviser. When Elliot complained about having to "waste his time" taking humanities courses, his adviser said that he could sympathize with Elliot's problem because there was so much to cover in the field of physics that he had some doubt whether it could really be done in four undergraduate years. On the other hand, the adviser also pointed out that the college wanted to turn out graduates that are *generally and broadly* educated and that a person who has no knowledge or understanding of the humanities is not considered being generally educated. In the adviser's opinion, it was as important for students majoring in the sciences to take humanities courses as it was for humanities majors to take science courses.

As Elliot mulled over this statement, he realized that there was more to a college education than becoming a physicist. Therefore, he could see that some of his problems with respect to his course in English literature revolved around his own attitudes: "How can I develop an interest in literature?" "What is there in literature that might interest me?" "In what way will my attitudes toward the humanities interfere with my benefiting from this course?" "Just what *are* my attitudes toward literature?"

As well as these rather general problems, Elliot also thought of some specific ones: "How can I schedule my work in order to give enough time to English literature, which is going to require a great deal of reading, in addition to my courses in science?" "What can I do to make literature courses more interesting?" "Is there any possible way that science and literature can be related?" "Will the techniques that I have used in other courses help me in literature courses?"

Problems in the first encounter. Although there was little that Elliot could actually do about taking action on any of these problems before the course got under way, he nevertheless found it helpful to ponder these issues. What had seemed like a dreary bore of a requirement began to take on possibilities that were challenging and potentially interesting. Hence he approached the first meeting of the class in a mood characterized by anticipation, curiosity, and some degree of eagerness.

The instructor turned out to be a Mr. Koch, an earnest young man in his mid-twenties who was obviously ill at ease, who talked in a low voice, and who had an annoying habit of addressing his remarks to a spot on the back wall about five feet above the heads of his students. He relaxed only when he answered a question Elliot had asked him about the format of the papers they were to hand in. He looked at the class for the first time and began to talk about the importance of using their experiences with the assigned books as an opportunity to communicate. This seemed to be a subject in which he was more interested. When there were no more questions, he dismissed the class early, with an obvious sigh of relief.

Elliot was somewhat puzzled by this first encounter with Mr. Koch. He was disappointed that the instructor did not make more of an attempt to "sell" him on literature, but he was pleased that Mr. Koch seemed willing to answer questions. He could anticipate, however, that one of the major problems in the course would be, "How can I get Mr. Koch to talk about the course in a more interesting way?"

Problems in scheduling. Later in the day, Elliot sat down at his desk and did some rough estimates of what his various courses would require of him. English literature was the first course of the day, at 8 o'clock. Chemistry was at 10, with a laboratory on Monday and Wednesday afternoons. Physics was at 11, with laboratory on Tuesday and Thursday afternoons. Math was at 1, and physical education was at 2 on Tuesdays and Thursdays, before the physics laboratory. Study time obviously had to be fitted in and around class and lab times. Using information he had on the first batch of assignments, coupled with his past experiences in science and math courses, he roughed out a schedule for the first two weeks. During Elliot's first term at college, he had found that it was impossible to make a schedule that could be followed exactly, because the demands of some courses tended to be heavier at some times of the term than at others. He had discovered, instead, that the practice of scheduling his time two weeks in advance, but also making a new and revised schedule each week, was the most practical. This approach enabled him to anticipate important future events, like examinations and due dates for papers, and to budget his time accordingly.

Another device that Elliot learned during his first two terms was that of "overanticipating" deadlines. If a report was due, say, on Wednesday the 12th, he scheduled its completion for Monday the 10th. Although the Monday deadline was a pretense, he worked as though the paper were actually due on that date. There were several advantages to this device. For one thing, he found himself actually under less pressure, because he knew that he had the two-day period as insurance. Because the pressure level was lower, he was able to do a less hurried job. On one occasion, he was happy that he had set an early deadline, because his parents unexpectedly dropped in for a visit, and he lost a Sunday afternoon for which he had scheduled library research. On another occasion, a bout of flu caused him to lose the better part of two days. Elliot was proud of the fact that his "flexible scheduling" had enabled him to get through three semesters without his having missed a deadline.

Problems in motivation. Flexible scheduling and overanticipation of deadlines were the major devices that enabled Elliot to deal with the problem of fitting his course in English literature into a crowded schedule. Problems of motivation were another matter. The course began with Beowulf and Chaucer. Elliot had no background for this material and he found it confusing, although he was reading Beowulf in translation and the passages from Chaucer were heavily footnoted. He dealt with these problems by talking to other students in the class about their ideas and interpretations with respect to the assigned readings. The first four students that Elliot talked to were noncommittal and offhand in their replies, but the fifth student turned out to be another science major, Peter Reyes, who had interests and problems similar to Elliot's. Peter and Elliot decided to have coffee after each class and talk over some of the difficulties they were encountering in the course. They found this discussion interesting and helpful because they not only were able to compare the notes they had taken in class but also were able to discuss and clarify points that were puzzling. Both Peter and Elliot regretted the occasional need to miss these talks when other assignments became more pressing.

A number of other developments resulted from this after-class interaction. Elliot and Peter began to ask questions and bring up points in class. Mr. Koch welcomed these interruptions and often seemed more eager to speak on the points they had brought up than to stick to his prepared lecture notes. They also talked with him after class and during his office hours. The instructor was even more relaxed on these occasions than he was in class, and his explanations seemed more understandable.

Thus Elliot used two strategies in dealing with his motivational problems in English literature. The first strategy was that of finding a fellow student who had similar interests and with whom he could discuss the course. These conversations gradually developed an attraction of their own, in the sense that it was interesting to talk to someone who had just been through the same experiences and to get his perspectives on what had occurred. The second strategy consisted of reducing some of the psychological distance between him and the instructor. Mr. Koch was a shy man who worked hard at preparing material for his course, but he was ill at ease in presenting it. The questions asked by Eliott and Peter made it possible for him to be more informal and relaxed, and he was, needless to say, rather pleased that students would show an interest in what he was presenting. Their discussion of the course with him after class also helped reduce the distance between them. Not only did they gain a better understanding of the issues in question but they were also able to get an idea of how he perceived English literature. This experience stood them in good stead during examinatons. Mr. Koch's questions tended to be rather involved and complex. A number of the other students had difficulties with the examinations because they were not sure what the instructor wanted in the way of an answer. Elliot and Peter had much less difficulty because their after-class discussions, their questions in class, and their informal contacts with the instructor had enabled them to grasp Mr. Koch's aims and interests. Therefore, they were better able to understand what he intended by the questions he asked.

Not all of Elliot's strategies worked. He still saw little or no relationship between his readings in literature and his science courses. He did find that some of what he had learned in previous English courses taken in high school and as a college freshman was helpful, and he often was able to recall half-forgotten bits of information. His most fruitful strategies, however, were those that enabled him to gain new perspectives on the course itself.

Steps in problem solving. There is some virtue in analyzing the problem-solving approach to learning in terms of steps, although few students (if any) actually follow these steps in a one–two–three order. The advantage in such a breakdown is that it enables us to get a bird's-eye view of the process and to discuss various aspects of it. In sequential order, here are the steps that most persons go through in solving a problem:

1. Recognizing and defining the problem.
2. Selecting appropriate strategies.
3. Testing or trying out strategies.
4. Evaluating results.
5. Revising strategies.

Recognizing and defining problems. As we noted previously, the first major step is that of recognizing and defining the problem, both in its general, long-range terms as well as in its specific and immediate terms. The task here is really that of deciding what the *crucial* problems are. In Elliot's case, the crucial problems were those of time and motivation, but another student might have different priorities. For example, his problem might be that of learning new methods and techniques. Problems of time and motivation, are, however, virtually universal, and all students must cope with them at some time or other.

Selecting appropriate strategies. Strategies should be appropriate to the problems they are designed to solve. Elliot used flexible scheduling and overanticipation of deadlines in dealing with his time problem. Other students might find that a more rigid and specific approach to scheduling works better. But strategies cannot solve all "time" problems. Consider, for example, the student who works thirty hours a week, who is on the basketball team, and who tries to carry a full academic load. It is not surprising that he can cope with his difficulties only by cutting classes and by trying to bluff his way through examinations because of lack of time to study. Motivation is really the basic problem here: for instance, Why does he cut his classes but never basketball practice? Why is he frequently late turning in an assignment but seldom late for work? It is clear where the priorities lie for him.

Strategies that deal with motivation should be selected with the interests of the student in mind. Elliot hit upon the idea of working with a fellow student because he enjoys talking with other students. A shyer student might have developed a strategy concerned with the assigned readings—perhaps outlining or writing questions for himself to answer. Students who recognize motivation as a problem and who select strategies accordingly, often begin by organizing or reorganizing the subject matter. This kind of strategy certainly has its advantages. Elliot achieved much the same result—a better understanding of English literature—through his conversations with Peter. The important gain in any successful strategy is the feeling of confidence and interest that results. Designing and carrying out strategies is a way of proving to oneself that the problem *can* be solved, and developing a plan to cope with a problem makes it more interesting than merely floundering helplessly. The problems posed by the courses that students take inevitably arouse some anxiety—there is no doubt about that. We can cope with this anxiety by one of the usual defense mechanisms —procrastination, rationalizing, or whatever—or we can deal with it by becoming involved in solving course-related problems. This involvement not only leads to the problem's solution but it also reduces our anxiety.

Testing or trying out strategies. The testing or trying out of strategies is a step that often takes place simultaneously with their selection. It may even occur while we are defining a problem. What happens is that while we are becoming aware of a problem we are at the same time developing a strategy to deal with it. In fact, we may be aware of a problem only after we have developed a strategy. We described Elliot's search for a study partner as an aftereffect of his being aware of some confusion about the course. Actually, he probably did not become aware of the points that were bothering him until he had mentioned them to other students. It was not, however, until Peter responded positively that Elliot got the idea that this might be a good way to study.

Many strategies develop in this more- or -less accidental way (which is not as accidental as it appears), since the student is actively working on a solution and is improvising by using elements from the situation as he encounters them.

Evaluating results. The proof of the pudding lies in the answer to the question: Do the strategies work? If the course becomes more interesting, if progress is being made, if the instructor's perspectives become more apparent—then the strategies are probably working. Sometimes they do not work. Louise Pichot is using a strategy similar to that of Elliot in her history class—that is, she is discussing the course with another student. She is now making low C's in the quizzes, whereas she was making D's, but that does not satisfy her. Since she is spending three hours a week in these conversations, she feels she should be showing more progress. This strategy is not working very well. She decides that she should spend more time with the books on the reading list. Thus far, she has read only those that are "absolutely required" and has not dipped into those marked "strongly recommended." She and her study partner decide that they will do more reading and will meet only once a week to compare notes.

Revising strategies. One has to maintain a flexible position with respect to strategies and be willing to revise and discard them if necessary. Students characteristically try several types of strategy during their first two or three terms at college and then settle on a few that seem to work and that are attuned to their interests and needs. What often happens, however, is that they get into courses where their favorite strategies do not work, and they are at a loss as to how to deal with this situation. Strategies that work with lecture-examination courses do not work well with discussion-term paper courses. Strategies that work with formal, "highly structured" instructors do not work well with informal, "unstructured" teachers. With the great variety of instructional styles that professors use today, students must be prepared to adapt their strategies accordingly.

Strategies as games. One of the problems in planning and selecting strategies that will enable us to maximize the gains to be made from the college experience is that of developing new perspectives on what learning involves. Without new perspectives, we are likely to fall into the trap of laying plans along lines that are familiar and comfortable for us but that are likely to be unproductive. One way of restructuring learning tasks is that of viewing them as a kind of game.

Hal Major is a business administration student who uses the games approach or, as he prefers to call it, "gamesmanship." Hal got this idea from some of his courses in business administration in which students play a kind of business game that includes many elements from real-life situations: financial resources, marketing problems, personnel with various kinds and levels of qualifications, and the like. After completing one of these courses, it occurred to Hal that succeeding in college also had many of the aspects of a game. For one thing, students, like players, can win or lose. Both types of activity also have rules and requirements, with penalties for infractions. There is a degree of competition in both, as well

43

as some element of chance. Players have a better chance to win games and students have a better chance to succeed in college if they plan and follow strategies that take all relevant factors into account.

Hal perceives the college situation as a kind of game in which he has two sets of "opponents": other students and the faculty. Perhaps "opponents" is the wrong word, because the education game can usually be played in such a way that everyone wins something and no one has to lose. This can occur when all students play the game according to the rules set by the instructor. In most instances, however, there are some students who do not observe the rules because they are unaware of them, or are aware of them and prefer not to follow them, refusing to recognize the instructor's right to set rules. Part of the problem facing each student-player is that of finding out what the rules are and adapting his behavior accordingly. Hal maintains that it is important to do this, because the instructor and only the instructor can determine whether a student player has won and how much he has won. It is ridiculous, he says, to pretend that rules do not exist or that they can be broken with impunity. He says that students often fail because they believe that the game can be played according to *their* rules and not those of the instructor. Hal has got into a number of arguments over this point with other students, who maintain that students have just as much right to set rules as instructors do. This line of reasoning never fails to irritate Hal, because he says it is irrelevant: there is no point in debating whether instructors have the right to set rules, because the reality of the situation is that the *instructors* set the rules.

Hal's strategy is somewhat like Elliot's. When he begins a course, he devotes considerable time to determining what the rules of the game are, what kinds of moves pay off, and what kinds do not. All courses, he says, are actually a series of subgames. Every class session is a subgame, as is every assignment and every examination or quiz. Ever since Hal has discovered this "gamesmanship" approach to college success, he has become somewhat of a bore: he goes around telling anyone who will listen how much difference it has made in his whole approach to his studies. His grades have gone up, he fells more at ease in class discussions, and he no longer suffers from "test nerves." All examinations are, he says, essentially games played between instructor and students. Although the instructor has all the trump cards, students can play the game to win, and most instructors will *help* students win if the student will observe the rules and will make it clear to the instructor what he is interested in winning.

When Hal described his games approach to Sally Stoltz, she said that she could never use it, because it sounded cynical and that furthermore it made college seem unimportant and trivial. She said that she didn't see how any student who took his work seriously could learn better if he pretended that he was involved in a game. Hal took exception to this objection. He said that he was just as serious about college and learning as any student and that he only used the gamesmanship strategy because it helped him develop a more objective view of things. He not only felt less tense and anxious about his classes but he also felt more equality with his instructors and hence better able to learn from them.

I have used Hal as my mouthpiece in presenting the games approach to learning because it *is* rather controversial. It certainly is not suited to every student. Some, like Sally, will say that it makes a mockery out of something that is very serious. Others will say that they would be unable to adopt the game pretense with anything that is as important to them as succeeding in college. Still others say that the games player is likely to focus on the superficial aspects of the college experience. There is the risk, of course, of following the game theory to its ultimate conclusion and deciding that because succeeding in college is "only a game," it is not worth playing.

The games approach would probably be attractive only to the students who enjoy "restructuring" complex social situations (like those involving college survival) and using their new perspectives to advantage. This approach may help these students become more objective about their relations with the instructor and fellow students and may also increase their interest and morale. Learning tasks can be tedious at times, and if they can be restructured in such a way as to make them less routine and more interesting, certainly nothing has really been lost.

Our approaches to learning, however, are likely to be personal, individual, and unique. There are many ways in which the learning situation can be restructured to permit new perspectives and new understandings of the relationship between oneself and the problem at hand. The games approach is only one way to restructure, and my chief purpose in presenting it here is not so much to recommend it but, instead, to show a way in which restructuring can be accomplished.

PERSONAL QUALITIES AND THE USE OF STRATEGIES

Students who stay in college versus dropouts. It is appropriate, here, to examine some of the factors—most of them psychological or emotional—that keep students from developing the kind of strategies that will enable them to benefit from the college experience. Some clues can be found by comparing the background of people who drop out of college with that of those who stay in and eventually get their degrees.

What psychologists call "task-orientation" seems to be an important characteristic. People who rate high on this factor seem to have less difficulty in applying themselves to tasks than do those who rate low. They enjoy being busy and occupied and are often restless if they are not involved in something useful. We would expect, therefore, that students rating high in task orientation would be able to identify problems, develop successful strategies, and thus be able to complete college requirements for a degree.

Some research by Alfred B. Heilbrun, Jr. (1965) suggests that this is indeed the case. Heilbrun administered a test of psychological needs to the entire freshman class at the University of Iowa. A year later he compared the scores of those who had dropped out of school with the scores of those who continued. He found that students who had remained in college tended to have stronger needs to achieve and to become involved in situations that require both a sense of order and the capacity to persist at a task in spite of distractions. These qualities of achievement, order, and persistence are very similar to the characteristic of task orientation I mentioned above. Heilbrun also found that students who remained in college had a greater need to defer to authorities and to respond favorably to encouragement, sympathy, and affection from others.

Heilbrun's data showed that students who dropped out tended to be more nonconforming than those who remained in college. The dropouts also showed stronger needs to dominate, to attract attention to themselves, and to behave in aggressive ways toward others. They were, in effect, less inclined to commit themselves to tasks, particularly to those that had been assigned by persons in authority. In a word, they were less *socialized* than were the students who stayed in college.

One of the unfaced problems of the students who dropped out seems to have been either that of refusing to recognize the realities of the college situation or that of developing ways of dealing with them effectively.

Personal qualities associated with academic success. Other research has produced results similar to that of Heilbrun. A study by John L. Holland (1959) of college students who had made outstanding scores on the National Merit Scholarship Examination found that those who later made the best grades in college rated higher on responsibility, self-control, and "socialization" than those who made poorer grades. In the test used by Holland, high scorers in "socialization" (not the some as "sociability") are described by the test manual as being:

Serious, honest, industrious, modest, obliging, sincere, and steady; as being conscientious and responsible; and as being self-denying and conforming (Gough, 1957).

Holland's findings are especially interesting because they show that students scoring high in traits like sociability, self-acceptance, and self-assurance, which are usually associated with good psychological adjustment, tended to get *lower* grades than students scoring low in these same traits. Therefore, when we speak of being *socialized,* we are talking about the qualities that are basic to performance and achievement in *learning* tasks rather than in group situations. It seems that the student who is less sure of himself and who is hence more willing to learn has a better chance of succeeding in college than the student who has poise, is self-assured, and is socially competitive. The student who is socially successful may thus have more of a problem in developing the kind of strategies that lead to academic success than the less popular student.

Two things should be noticed here: (1) the results of both the Heilbrun and Holland studies apply to students who are academically very able, and may have less relevance to students in the middle and lower ranges of academic ability; and (2) the studies report *trends* and not absolutes. Many bright students who are socially aggressive succeed, and many who are modest and retiring fail. The *general tendency,* however, appears to favor students who are less dominant and nonconforming and more willing to cooperate with teachers and other authority figures.

Strategies used by successful and unsuccessful students. Let me introduce the findings of a study that I conducted with my assistants,[1] a study to which I shall refer from time to time throughout this book. We were interested in finding out some of the ways in which more successful students differ from less successful ones. The target groups in this study consisted of one sample of 40 undergraduate students at San Francisco State College whose grades averaged B or better and another sample of equal size who were averaging C minus or poorer. We thus deliberately excluded the "typical" student whose average grades range from a B minus down to a low C because we wanted to identify the attitudes and behaviors that contribute most significantly to academic success or

[1] Margaret Black and Marilyn Wilson.

failure. San Francisco State College is an ideal place to conduct such a study because its student body is "average" in a number of ways. It offers a full range of academic majors and attracts students from a variety of backgrounds. Furthermore, the academic ability of its average students, as measured by college aptitude tests, is fairly close to the average for colleges throughout the country.

The method we used was that of having graduate research assistants interview each student in the two groups individually and ask them about their approaches to learning tasks. This technique differed from the one usually used in study methods research: that is, administering questionnaires to a large number of students whose replies are then classified according to their grade-point averages. Inasmuch as the interviewers in this study were themselves students, we thought that the students in the two groups would be more likely to be frank about the techniques they were using, as well as their attitudes and feelings about studying.

Our first finding was concerned with the relationship between study techniques and motivation:

Reasons given by successful students for their success		*Reasons given by unsuccessful students for their lack of success*	
Good study habits	33%	Lack of study	25%
Interest	25	Lack of interest	35
Intelligence	15	Personal problems	8
Family influence	5	Other	32
Other	22		

The successful students attributed their success mainly to two factors: the way in which they went about the tasks of studying and their motivation. The same two factors were also prominent in a negative way in the explanations given by less successful students. Their reports strongly supported what we have already suggested about success in college: the kind of motivation students have is as important, if not more important, as the methods they use in studying.

The second finding is particularly relevant to our discussion.

49

Here are the differences between the two groups with respect to the way in which they scheduled their time during the week.

Type of schedule	Successful	Unsuccessful
Detailed, "strict"	38%	38%
Loose, flexible	30	5
None	32	57

The approach used by the successful students is more in keeping with the problem-solving approach I have described. About two thirds of the successful students used some type of scheduling, as contrasted with less than half the unsuccessful ones. The important difference between the two groups, however, is found in the use of flexible scheduling, since the same proportion of the two groups employed a detailed and "strict" type of scheduling. In other words, loose, flexible scheduling is much more characteristic of successful students than of unsuccessful ones, whereas the use of detailed, "strict" scheduling offers no particular advantage, inasmuch as unsuccessful students were as likely to use this approach as were successful ones.

The majority of instructors at San Francisco State College, as in most colleges today, do not grade on the basis of class attendance, and students are thus relatively free to make the decision as to whether they will attend class. Therefore the extent to which a student attends class may be considered as a kind of index to the extent of his commitment to the educational process. The answers to questions about attendance also showed a major difference between the successful and the unsuccessful students:

Class Attendance	Successful	Unsuccessful
Always or almost always	85%	48%
Sometimes absent	8	8
Often absent	8	45

It is probably not crucial whether a student misses or attends a class, but the attitudes that he has toward attendance do appear

50

to be crucial. These figures show that almost twice as many successful students as unsuccessful ones were scrupulous about attendance and that more than five times as many unsuccessful as successful students had poor attendance. The student who accepts the challenge of the college situation, and who sees the tasks of learning as problems to be solved, is much more likely to perceive class attendance as helping him solve these problems. Not only is he more likely to keep current with assignments, date changes for papers and exams, and the like, but he is also in a better position to become involved in the subject he is studying and to understand the instructor's attitudes and approaches to the problems at hand. Attendance records are therefore indicative of the kind of attitude students have toward the subject, the instructor, and education in general. Consequently, attendance can be an index to both motivation and morale. The student who finds reasons for not going to class is beginning to fail, if he has not failed already. Indeed, poor class attendance is one of the first signs of a student's decision to drop out. Interestingly, these signs may appear before the student is aware that he has made this decision.

The results of the San Francisco State College survey show that successful and unsuccessful students do differ in terms of the basic strategies they use in their approach to their college work. When the findings of this study are taken together with the other research we presented, however, it appears that the underlying issue is probably one of motivation. Students with strong needs to achieve, who are "task-oriented," or who relate well to persons in authority, find it easier to design strategies that succeed than do students who are nonconforming, socially aggressive, or popular with their group. Although there is no particular reason why students who are socially active cannot develop and make use of problem-solving strategies in attaining satisfactory levels of academic success, it seems obvious that their interests and orientation to life expose them to distractions that make it more difficult for them to do so. The word is "difficult," however, not "impossible."

CHAPTER FOUR

Learning: an adventure in communication (I)

IF listening to lectures and reading are learning, how can they also be communication?

ARE fast readers really the best readers?

How can reading murder mysteries and westerns help students with reading problems?

WHAT happens to students who try to compete with the instructor?

SHOULD lecture notes be extensive or brief?

WHAT can you do to fight the law of gravity on the ski slope of a forgetting curve?

The importance of communication. Peter F. Drucker (1952), a specialist in human relations in industry, once said that the most valuable basic skill taught in college is the ability to organize and express ideas in writing and in speaking.

Although everyone would agree that most students do not learn this basic skill as adequately as they should, the fact remains that college graduates, on the whole, express themselves more effectively than those who have not had the benefit of a college education. Some college graduates are more competent in this respect than others, of course, and those who are most competent are likely to be more successful in whatever enterprise they undertake than those who are less competent.

Input, output, and feedback. Being able to express oneself in writing and speaking is, however, only one aspect of communication. As far as most people are concerned, speaking and writing *are* communication. Perhaps this essentially one-dimensional view of communication results from the fact that difficulties in self-expression are so frustrating and annoying. When someone says to us, "You are not communicating very well," we are inclined to take ourselves to task for not stating things more clearly, overlooking the fact that the problem may lie in some other aspect of communication, such as the kind of information we are trying to communicate, or the readiness of our audience to receive information, rather than in our ability to express ourselves. If we wish to communicate more effectively, we should look at some of its other dimensions.

One way to look at communication is to borrow a concept from what psychologists call *open-systems theory*, a theory that has been used to understand and explain the operation of a wide variety of *systems,* both animate and inanimate, ranging from atoms and one-celled animals to computers and human beings. Any individual may be thought of as a system that is affected by its environment and which, in turn, also has an effect on the environment. Whatever the individual receives from the environment may be called *inputs,* and whatever he produces or does may be called *outputs.* The changes in the environment that result from output may also be reported back to the individual as *feedback*. In this discussion, we are concerned only with that type of behavior called communication, although open-systems theory may be applied to all other types of behavior as well.

Output in communication includes speaking, but it also includes other forms of self-expression. Writing papers, making reports, participating in class discussions, and giving reports are all forms of output, but so is taking examinations. Anything that a student does to indicate attitudes and feelings is a form of output. For instance, looking out of the window while the instructor is making a particular point during a lecture is a form of output, because it is a way of showing lack of interest. Output may also take the form of frequent absence from class or habitual tardiness—both nonverbal forms of expressing lack of interest or dislike of the course or the instructor. Conversely, stopping after class to listen to the instructor clear up a difficult point for another student is a nonverbal way of showing interest.

The input aspect of communication includes reading, listening, and note-taking. Unless this aspect is developed, the communicator, or student, literally would have nothing to communicate and no knowledge of the symbols and concepts that make self-expression possible.

Feedback is a term that is applied to a group of processes characterized by both output and input and that include evaluation, self-testing, and checking out one's impressions and concepts with the instructor, other students, or any other person competent to give an opinion. Feedback is, essentially, a kind of followup. The individual passes on information to others, and checks to see whether the audience (person or persons who receive the communication) has understood the message. He is also, of course, interested in the kind of impression the message made on the audience—for instance, whether it achieved its intended effect or whether it went wide of the mark.

I have presented these three aspects of communication as though they were separate functions, yet they ordinarily operate together and may even be difficult to distinguish from one another. As George writes his paper (output) he reads it back to himself (input) and

55

tries to imagine what effect it will have on the instructor (feedback). When he participates in a class discussion (output), he listens (input) to what others say, and notes how his ideas are received (feedback).

Since we are continually involved in one or more aspects of communication, we tend to take communication for granted and are not deeply concerned about our effectiveness as communicators until we experience an obvious misunderstanding. Most of the time, however, we are not communicating as effectively as we should, usually because we are preoccupied with one dimension of communication to the exclusion of others. It is because communication is so vital in educational success and because it is generally carried on so ineffectively that I am devoting this entire chapter to the subject.

INPUT

Reading: the need for speed. The two major input activities in college are reading and listening. Both are important, but reading probably is the more crucial of the two skills. More of a student's time is likely to be spent in reading than in any single type of learning activity, and inability to read effectively is probably the greatest hidden cause of college failure. Here is an example of this.

Students often come to see me when they have received low scores on their midterm examinations. A student will usually say that he cannot understand how he happened to do so badly, because he was most conscientious and spent many hours going over his textbook. It is my practice on these occasions to telephone the college testing office and request the score the student made on the reading test he took as part of the battery of entrance tests. Almost without fail I find that he scored well below the average for college applicants. When I tell the student that his chief problem seems to be that of a deficiency in reading, he is genuinely puzzled. "But I read so carefully," he says, and shows me the underlined passages in his textbook that indicate how he has read and re-read it. Then I try to explain that it is not enough to read carefully, that he must also read rapidly. He is confused by this, because common sense tells him that a fast reader cannot be a good reader. Yet the research findings are crystal clear on this point: fast readers have a better understanding of what they have read than poor readers. The slow reader gets lost in the details of what he is trying to read; it is the old story of not seeing the forest for the trees.

At this juncture I usually point out that students who are slow readers are at a great disadvantage in college. Colleges today require students to do a great deal of reading. In order to collect material for a term paper, a student must cover a vast amount of material very rapidly. A reading method that is very useful in such assignments is *scanning*: running the eye rapidly over thousands of words, looking for key words that identify items of possible interest. Material covered by the scanning method may include reference guides, library index cards, abstracts, and books and journals of all types. Only when the student notices something interesting does he stop and shift over to another style of reading. He will then probably read the passage in question more intensively, but still very rapidly, in order to determine whether it actually is the kind of thing he is looking for. If so, then he will read it once more, shifting to a slower, more deliberate kind of reading, in order to get the full import of the material.

The student thus needs to have a flexible approach to reading: he must vary his approach in accordance with his objective in reading, as well as with the kind of material he is reading. A light novel will, of course, call for a reading approach different from that used with a detailed description of the methods employed in a scientific experiment. The rapid reader generally has this flexibility because he can read slowly whenever he wishes; the slow reader, however, is unable to modify his approach because he has been unable to increase his rate beyond the word-for-word level.

Students who can only read slowly are also at a marked disadvantage when it comes to taking objective tests—that is, tests of a true-false, multiple-choice, matching, or short-answer type. A typical multiple-choice examination may consist of fifty items to be completed in a fifty-minute period. This is ample time for the average college student, but the slow reader characteristically takes about forty minutes to cover the first twenty-five items and then finds that he has only ten minutes in which to do the last half of the test.

Enjoyment of reading. Usually, but not always, the slow reader is a reluctant reader. When I ask him what he does in his leisure time—week ends, summers, and on holidays—he may list a variety of activities: swimming, skiing, talking to friends, working with hobbies, watching television, but *not* reading. People whose idea of fun is relaxing with a good book tend to read it rapidly. After all, there are so many interesting books to read, and if you spend too much time on any one of them, you are missing opportunities to enjoy the others. Consequently, I advise slow readers to start reading for enjoyment, to begin with news magazines, digests, murder mysteries, auto racing magazines—it does not matter, as long as they get involved in reading and develop an active interest in it. A certain amount of time, I tell them, should be spent reading things they enjoy, in order to reinforce the reading habit.

Remedial measures. Many colleges, particularly at the junior college level, provide remedial reading courses. Some of them are taught by instructors who have developed a high degree of skill in helping students improve speed and comprehension; there is, however, a shortage of such instructors, and many remedial courses are taught by less-experienced faculty members. But students who are slow readers cannot afford to pass up any opportunity to improve their skill, and those that I have referred to remedial courses in which the instruction was only mediocre have made good gains, as long as they were conscientious and willing to persist. In recent years a number of private, off-campus "reading institutes" or "reading clinics" have been advertising that, for a fee, they will teach anyone how to speed up his reading. Students of mine who have patronized these clinics generally report good results.

A student can, of course, increase his reading speed by working on his own. There are a number of texts that any librarian will be glad to locate for interested students, and college bookstores sometimes carry manuals devoted to developing reading skill. Even if special courses or texts are not available, a student can set aside one or two half-hour periods a day for reading improvement, setting himself a steadily increasing quota of pages to be read per hour.

One effective method that is taught in some reading clinics is that of using the index finger to pace the eyes. Other experts recommend the use of a 3 x 5 index card that is moved down the page, pausing briefly to expose each line. Both of these methods enable the student to speed up the pace of his reading, to prevent regression (going back over material already covered), and to enhance interest and involvement in the reading task. These pacing devices also increase the *activity* of the student. They involve him in the task and help him resist distraction.

Comprehension usually improves along with speed, but students who have never done much reading may also have problems with vocabulary. A common practice is that of keeping a notebook of words whose meaning presents difficulties. This approach is particularly helpful in fields that have a large number of technical words with which students are unfamiliar.

The chief problem with any self-help method is that of self-discipline and persistence. If we have signed up for a remedial course or paid a fee at a reading clinic, we are more likely to follow through and complete the assignments. Most of us, however, find it difficult to follow a routine or regimen that we have set for ourselves, particularly if the activity is distasteful or tedious. It is easier to accomplish the goal of an improved skill or competence if we get the support and the reinforcement of a special instructor and a group of fellow students who are also interested in improving their reading.

Studying. The word *studying,* as far as most students are concerned, means reading the textbook in a way that maximizes retention of facts. Indeed, many students think that reading is all there is to studying. There is no doubt that the ability to read and retain information in a textbook is crucial in courses that focus on the information included between the covers of one or two text-books, but the overall percentage of these courses has been declining in colleges and universities for some years. An increasing number of courses, particularly in the junior and senior years, require the student to become familiar with a wide variety of sources: for example, scientific and scholarly journals, monographs, and pamphlets, whereas textbooks, if any, are relegated to a less prominent role. In spite of this trend, however, students in the typical introductory course are expected to become familiar with the contents of the assigned textbook. The need to attain a high degree of familiarity with the contents of textbooks has led to the publication of many "how to study" manuals, each with its formula for obtaining maximum retention as efficiently as possible.

These formulas have a number of points in common. They usually recommend that the student should first survey the material to be mastered in order to get a general idea of what he is to cover. This overview should include the notation of section headings and lead sentences and—this is most essential—the reading of any summary material, such as that found at the end of chapters in many textbooks. It is also a good idea to read over any end-of-chapter questions at this point, because they not only show the topics that are brought up in a chapter but they also serve to raise the interest level of what the student is about to read. In other words, the material to be covered makes better sense and is more interesting if the student is looking for answers to real questions. Too much of what students have to read consists of answers to questions that they have not yet asked themselves. If there are no ready-made questions at the chapter end, the student is encouraged to write a few of his own, in order to facilitate this question-and-answer process.

The next step in these study formulas consists of a fairly intensive reading of the material contained in the chapter. A number of techniques may be useful at this juncture. Some students are helped by marking particularly significant passages. This can, of course, be overdone when more sentences are marked or under-lined than not. Marking can also be helpful when it is used to highlight key ideas that may be identified when time for review is at hand.

The method that most students have found to be useful is that of using a marking pen to lay a cover of a light, transparent color—yellow, for example—on the line of print that is to be emphasized. This method is better than underlining because the color keeps the student's point of attention on the line itself and not below it. The color also makes the emphasized material stand out dramatically from the rest of the page. Marking pens can also be used to make notes on the margin of a book for the purpose of directing attention to a sequence of points, a new word, a definition, or a statement of a principle or law.

Some students will not mark a book because they want to preserve its resale value. If this kind of student learns best by underlining or color marking, such a policy is short-sighted. He invests time worth hundreds of dollars in a course and then, to save three or four dollars, refuses to use a study technique that would help him derive benefit from that investment. Some students, to be sure, do not need to mark up a book and, instead, study by jotting down an outline on another sheet of paper as they read along.

It really does not matter what method is used, as long as the student involves himself *actively* in the task of learning from a textbook and organizes the material in some way that makes sense to him. Hence it is unwise penny-pinching to buy books that are already underlined or color-marked. The work is already done, and the student does not get a chance to involve himself actively. Unless students can make use of some device such as those I have described, reading becomes a passive activity—all input and no output. Learning, as noted previously, succeeds only to the extent that the student actively participates in the process. Underlining, color marking, question posing, and outlining are useful to the extent that they get the student involved in the learning process. If the student becomes involved, the material to be covered becomes *his*. Otherwise, it remains *theirs*—something that pertains to the author or the instructor, but certainly not to him.

The exact technique used by a student in reading a textbook is not important, as long as he uses some method that works for him. It should be a matter of personal preference which system is used. Outlining is obviously a preferred method for students who cannot bring themselves to mark up a textbook. Others prefer underlining because it seems to have a here-and-now reinforcement effect. Probably students should experiment with a number of different approaches before settling on one that seems to yield the best results.

The third phase in the formulas recommended by the how-to-study manuals consists of some kind of review of what has been read. This may consist of going back to the questions that were originally posed and trying to answer them. A question that cannot be answered naturally suggests that some vital points were missed in the reading. The intensity of this review is determined in part by the expectations of the instructor. The more detailed his demands, the more intensive the review. If, on the other hand, the student is more interested in general principles, he can concentrate on a restatement of the main points covered. Actually, the restatement of main points is essential under *both* conditions, because details make better sense when they are related to an overall structure than if they consist of unorganized bits of specific information.

How-to-study manuals also emphasize the need to review after a lapse of time. As many a student has found to his sorrow, the slope of the forgetting curve is precipitous. Recall is excellent ten minutes after a chapter has been read. A few hours later, some of the details have already slipped away, and a few days later probably most of what has been so painfully learned has been forgotten. All is not lost, however. A rapid review, which should take much less time than the first reading, ought to bring the forgotten details back to mind. If retention over a period of time is important, the student must be willing to follow a schedule of periodic review.

Students tend to believe that learning will automatically take place if they follow some kind of regimen like that which I have just described. Whether the plan is successful, however, depends on the attitudes and feelings students bring to the task. They can, for example, effectively sabotage their own efforts if chronic or acute feelings of hostility or resentment toward the instructor or the course prevent their involving themselves in the task at hand. The need to find some dimension of the task that arouses interest or involvement is so great that no effort should be spared to find any angle or aspect that makes the task more interesting or appealing. Here are some examples.

Selma Zorn resented her philosophy professor, Dr. Brock. In her opinion, he was opinionated, unwilling to listen to students, and arrogant. It seemed to her, furthermore, that his interpretations left much to be desired. As a way of proving to herself that she was right and he was wrong, she undertook a considerable amount of outside reading. She did not, of course, ask the instructor what to read, because she did not want to give him the satisfaction of helping her. Instead, she looked up her own sources with some help from the librarian. As a result, she became the best informed student in the class and ended up with the top grade. As she explained her success later, however, she said that she learned a great deal in Dr. Brock's course, but in *spite* of him rather than because of him.

Philip Hicks found his required course in zoology a bore. There was so much uninteresting material to be memorized. His girl friend, a science major, was also in the same class. She could not see why he was having problems, because she found the course fascinating. She was getting high B's and A's in the weekly quizzes, whereas Philip was getting low C's and D's. Philip, determined that he was not going to be shown up by a girl, set for himself the task of topping her quiz grades. He tackled the job of memorizing by organizing material into blocks and spending fifteen-minute periods memorizing three and four times a day. He prepared a pack of cards for the more difficult terms and carried them around with him. Whenever he had a few spare minutes, he pulled out his cards and did a quick review. If he knew a term, he would put it on the bottom of the pack. If he did not know it, he put it near the top. Within two weeks of initiating the new regimen, he was scoring near the top of the class on weekly quizzes. He never developed a real interest in zoology, but the task of learning became more interesting. Indeed, the card system worked so well that he used it with some success in a foreign-language course that he had to take a year later.

What Selma and Philip did in these learning situations is what is called *restructuring*—they changed the structure of the situation from one in which learning could not take place into one in which learning became both possible and actually interesting.

Lecture notes. Lectures are second only to books as major sources of communication input. Listening to lectures involves some skills that differ from those used in reading textbooks and some that are similar.

Differences arise, of course, because the input in the lecture situation is aural rather than visual. This introduces a disadvantage: the learner is usually unable to review the material in advance and, unless he takes excellent notes, is unable to do a complete review after the fact. But there are some advantages in the lecture situation that are not experienced in reading. The lecturer serves not only as a source of information but also as a kind of model with respect to attitudes toward the information and concepts he is discussing. His tone of voice, gestures, and facial expressions add dimensions of meaning that cannot be obtained from the printed page and that provide clues to the relative value and importance of the various topics being covered. There is often the opportunity to ask for clarification and to get puzzling questions resolved, an opportunity that is completely lacking when one reads a text. Instructors differ in their attitude toward such questions. Some permit interruptions, others refuse to answer questions until the end of the period, and still others do not allow them at all. When questions are not allowed, it is often possible to speak with the instructor after class or during his office hours to clear up difficult points. Most instructors welcome these indications of interest and are eager to clarify obscurities. A few will do so only reluctantly, however, and a student must be unusually persistent and patient in order to get the answers he is entitled to.

It is difficult to suggest or prescribe a set of techniques that can be used to get the most out of lectures. This is partly because objectives and styles of lecturers vary so widely. Some lecturers elaborate on the textbook; in these instances, the responsibilities of students are fairly limited. Other lecturers largely ignore the textbook and teach a course that is quite different in sequence and structure from the material assigned to be read. Under these circumstances, the student must, in effect, cope with two different courses: the one taught by the instructor and the one covered in the textbook.

It would help students to determine what role to play during the lecture period if they knew what the evaluation policies of the instructor were, and very often a kind of a game develops during the early weeks of the course in which students attempt to get the instructor to commit himslf on an evaluation policy, and the instructor, for one reason or another, makes statements that somehow leave students dissatisfied. They would like to know, for example, whether they are going to be examined on both the textbook and the lecture. Some instructors lecture, but only examine on the textbook. In such instances, they are understandably reluctant to say that the examinations will contain no questions on the lecture, because they will lose the attention (and perhaps the attendance) of students. Therefore they may say that attendance at lectures will *aid* the students in the examination. This is very likely true, because even if lectures are not directly related to the textbook, they do provide a frame of reference that enables the serious student to organize and conceptualize the material he reads and hence to understand it better. But students are likely to believe that if no test item relates *directly* to the lecture, the instructor is misleading them.

Another problem in instructor-student communication occurs when the instructor has not decided exactly how he will evaluate the learning taking place in his course. He has selected a textbook that represents some aspects of what he thinks is important in the course he is teaching, and he plans to deliver a series of lectures that covers other significant aspects. He has only a vague idea of how to evaluate student performance because he intends to develop his plans as he goes along.

These are but two examples of the reasons why it is often difficult for students to get firm information on what kind of evaluation will be made and "what I must study in order to pass the test." In a general way, all the student can really do under such circumstances is to accept the fact that any course is an adventure in learning, as well as in communication. Many instructors welcome the student's active participation in this adventure and are willing to include him as a participant in planning. In these instances, student suggestions will be eagerly received and acted upon. In other instances, the main direction of the venture will remain in the hands of the instructor and the student will function as an actively participating spectator to the unfolding of the course. This, too, can be an exciting experience.

Most how-to-study manuals contain directions on how to get the most out of lectures. They usually recommend brief, synoptic notes, preferably in outline form. Taking adequate notes requires a considerable degree of skill and practice. More than mere listening is required, because one must organize and summarize as the lecturer goes along. The basic problem seems to be this: the more extensive one's notes, the less one hears; and the more closely one listens, the more difficult it is to take adequate notes. The problem, in other words, seems to be that of striking a happy balance between taking too many or too few notes.

Most successful notetakers develop a system of abbreviations—essentially, their own brand of shorthand. Some systems, like Speedwriting, are ready-made and are easily learned from manuals. They enable the student to listen more attentively because the time spent in writing is kept to a minimum.

It is important to remember, however, that notes should be reviewed and, if possible, rewritten or retyped. The principle here is much the same as the one that applied to reading textual material: the review facilitates the involvement of the student and promotes retention. The greater the use of abbreviations or shorthand-like notes, the more desirable it is to redo notes after a lapse of no more than a few days. Students are often surprised to find that rewriting notes opens up new dimensions of understanding and that they actually understand the lecture better (say, three days later), when they review their notes, even though they had not been aware of any problems of communication at the time. The principle here is that rewriting lecture notes facilitates personal involvement, and both learning and communication are improved when students become involved.

Roger H. Garrison sums up these points very well:

To listen well is first to respond creatively within yourself. This requires at least as much energy from you as talking does; real attention is not passive.[1]

[1] *The adventure of learning in college.* New York: Harper, 1959.

CHAPTER FIVE

Learning: an adventure in communication (II)

OUTPUT

WHAT does writing a paper or taking an examination have to do with *real* learning?

How does poor grammar introduce "noise in the channel?"

IF a student has done an original and interesting piece of writing, is it reasonable for the instructor to be fussy about spelling?

WHY do good spellers make more use of the dictionary than poor spellers?

"IT's neat, it's nice, but it doesn't say anything." What can you do when instructors demand content?

How can a typewriter be used to reduce "noise in the channel?"

MANY class discussions are boring because they are monopolized by a few students. What can you do about this problem?

IN view of the fact that learning is hard, demanding work, is it fair for instructors to increase the stress on students by giving them examinations and grades?

The role of output in learning. There is a kind of folklore about learning that has developed over the centuries, a folklore that goes back at least to the days of the medieval universities. According to this folklore, learning consists of processes of absorption: reading, studying, and listening to lectures—the input side of communication. The active or output side, as represented by examinations and papers, is considered as having nothing to do with learning but, instead, is an unpleasant series of tasks that the student must perform at the command of the instructor; tasks that may actually *interfere* with learning. Input, according to this view, is something the student does for himself, whereas output is something the student does for the instructor.

Folklore does not, of course, come into being for no reason at all, and it is not very difficult to determine why students find it easy to favor input over output aspects of communication: a student who limits himself to input may or may not be learning and no one is the wiser. The student who engages in output—who has to "put it out," to use the popular phrase—must expose his work to the scrutiny of others. In other words, the quality of his output may enable instructors to find out that he has not been learning at all, but has merely been going through the motions. There is still a further hazard, one that arouses even more anxiety: the student may find *himself* out, and this is the greatest risk of all. Most of us have a subsurface, irrational fear that we are really stupid. We think that we have been successful in pretending that we are intelligent, but that some day we will do something that will prove beyond the shadow of doubt that our appearance of intelligence is really fraudulent. The only way we can preserve the illusion, we think, is to say or write as little as possible. Since normal functioning depends on self-confidence, we avoid anything that can possibly undermine it.

Our self-concept is the most vulnerable area in the self-structure, and we strive to protect it at all costs. It is embarrassing to reveal our shortcomings to others, but it is shattering when we have to face them ourselves. Many of the maneuvers that we think we undertake to avoid public embarrassment are actually done to preserve our own self-image.

Our self-image of the eager learner may be enhanced when we lug a pile of books home from the library. This behavior helps convince us and the casual observer as well. The fact that we can impress the observer helps reinforce our concept of ourselves as being studious, sincere, hardworking and conscientious. But learning is more than building a comfortable and satisfying image. What really counts is our ability to demonstrate that what we have learned has become a part of us. Output requires us to *use* what we have learned. If we cannot use it, we have not learned it.

The student's output, in the form of written or oral statements, shows his familiarity with the concepts of a special field, his ability to organize and relate concepts, his acquaintanceship with technical vocabularies, and the like. Students have a traditional resistance, however, to being asked to state, orally or in writing, what they have learned, and they often give rather elaborate arguments to avoid such assignments. They say, for example, that these tasks do not actually reveal what they have learned, that the assignments they are given represent inadequate samples of their competence in the field.

It is far too facile to say, as many instructors do, that students resist assignments because they are lazy. It may well be, of course, that instructors have encouraged students to play dependent and passive roles to the point where students have been led to believe that education is essentially a passive process. This may be true, but a further analysis of the problem suggests that the reluctance of students is related, as I have noted, to a fear of self-exposure. Educational practices are, unfortunately, mistake-oriented—that is, students are more likely to be criticized and penalized for their errors and shortcomings than they are to be praised and rewarded for their successes and strengths. It therefore takes a considerable degree of self-discipline and ego strength to overcome the reluctance to expose oneself by writing papers or making statements in class. Fortunately, most students are able to exercise this self-discipline at least some of the time.

Written assignments. We shall focus our attention here on assigned papers, and I shall discuss writing done during essay examinations in the next section on feedback.

Instructors usually provide more opportunities for students to express themselves in writing than in speaking. Hence writing skills contribute more to academic success as measured by grades than oral skills do. Most, but not all, students prefer to have their written rather than their spoken statements evaluated. A student who is given a written assignment does not have to expose his product until he has had a chance to organize it and work it over. Many students, unfortunately, do not take advantage of this opportunity and turn in papers that are hastily thrown together and that have not been edited for errors in grammar, punctuation, and spelling. When the instructor raises questions about these matters, the students tend to excuse such deficiencies on the ground that they should be judged on their *ideas,* not the form in which the ideas are stated. This argument comes under the heading of youthful rebelliousness and rejection of authority. After all, it is society that has set the standards for written expression, and these young people are announcing, in effect, that society's rules do not apply to them. Another type of problem is presented by students who turn in neatly typed papers, impeccable in form, that really do not say anything. The first type of student has something to say, but rejects the standards for written communication that have been set by the society and culture in which he holds membership; the second type accepts the formal requirements but dissociates himself from the need to say something.

A basic and unresolved problem for both types of students is their inability to perceive written assignments as opportunities to communicate with the instructor. It is helpful to view the student as an initiator of communication, a person who sends *information* by way of a communication channel to the instructor. In this instance, the assignment of the paper opens up the channel, and the *information* or *message* is the written paper and its contents. Students who are unaware that the assignment gives them an opportunity to reach the instructor with their messages may write something that misses the mark. They may not take into account the effect that their messages will have on the person receiving them.

Perhaps the point can be made more effectively by comparing written with oral communication. The student who is unconcerned about the requirements of form would be unlikely to address the instructor using words and grammatical terms that are bizarre and exotic to the extreme, because he would recognize that this unusual language would distract the instructor's attention from the content of his message. This is the chief reason for insisting on the usual amenities of form: deviations are distracting and confusing and they introduce what psychologists call "noise" (interference that reduces the intelligibility of the message) into the channels of communication. If the second type of student referred to above would also speak to the instructor along the lines of his written communication, he might recognize how rudimentary and banal his ideas are. "Noise" is not the problem with his message; instead, it is "content-free."

To return to the matter of using conventional forms in writing, the primary problem is not ability but *motivation*, since any student who is competent enough to gain admittance to a college is capable of using conventional forms in written communication. As Albert R. Kitzhaber (1963) says in his manual for college teachers of English, "It is hard to believe that students who are capable of learning physics and French, college algebra and economics, are not capable of studying a handbook by themselves to learn the rules for forming the possessive case or the correct preposition to use with 'different.'"

Handbooks of English usage and style manuals for proper forms to be used in writing papers are readily available in college bookstores, and students who have difficulties with the formal aspects of writing should keep them close at hand and refer to them frequently.

Spelling, of course, can be corrected by recourse to a dictionary. Contrary to popular opinion, it is the good spellers, not the poor ones, who make frequent use of dictionaries. Spelling can be learned just like any other skill but, again, motivation is the major difficulty. Recognizing that poor spelling *is* a handicap that must be overcome is the first step. The next step is that of following one of the procedures suggested in one of the several workbooks devoted to this problem. These techniques usually consist of making lists of "demons," or words most often misspelled, like "develop," "occurred" and "separate." Standard lists of prefixes and suffixes may also facilitate word analysis. If basic structure of compound words is understood, students are less likely to make spelling errors.

Kitzhaber's comments are also appropriate here:

> The sooner a student is persuaded of the enormous social importance of conventional spelling, the sooner he will take pains to eliminate misspellings from his work—and the sooner, perhaps, he will gain secure mastery over the spelling of the words he most often uses. The departmental rule should therefore be stringent, perhaps a failing grade for a three-page paper containing three or more separate misspellings. The rule might begin to apply with the third paper of the term, after students have been clearly and repeatedly warned.[1]

The student who has problems with spelling, grammar, and punctuation can derive considerable benefit from remedial instruction. Some colleges have "writing clinics" to which these students can be referred. One student in a college that had no remedial services solved his problem by hiring another student, an English major, to edit his themes. This decision had two results. First, his discussions and arguments with his "editor" got him interested in the problems of applying formal rules of expression which, in turn, proved to be a valuable experience in learning. Second, the fact that his writing deficiencies were costing him money out of his own pocket gave him a strong incentive to mend his ways. Within a few weeks he had dispensed with the special service and was doing his own editing.

[1] Reprinted (by permission) from *Themes, theories, and therapy: the teaching of writing in college.* New York: McGraw-Hill, 1963.

What this student learned to do was to assume, when he had written his first draft of a paper, that he had made errors. Many students are unwilling to face or admit this probability, and the draft they hand in to the instructor is their first one. The fact is, virtually no one turns out a finished product on his first try. The secret of good writing lies in assuming that one has made errors or used awkward phraseology and in revising and editing first and (hopefully) second drafts. To be sure, few students have the time to do three or four drafts of a paper, but only the student who is actively seeking a failing grade should attempt to palm off a first draft as a finished product.

In many ways the student who has mastered the formal aspects of writing but has nothing to say is in a more difficult position than those who cannot or will not revise and edit their written assignments. There are, after all, manuals to aid those whose main deficiencies are formal, but no manual can help the person whose writing is "content-free." His task is essentially that of becoming more closely identified with the subject at hand, of perceiving relationships between the subject matter and his own experience and background. This is the basic difficulty that I have mentioned a number of times previously: that of becoming less self-concerned and identifying more closely with the academic world. Most students cannot accomplish this change without a significant reorientation of their attitudes toward themselves and their social environment. It can be done, and many students do eventually make the change, but it is not an easy one.

A major failing of essays that are free of content is that the reader finds them uninteresting. Indeed, one has a hunch that the writer did not find them interesting either. It generally turns out that statements which the initiator finds uninteresting are also uninteresting to the receiver. One way to make papers interesting to the reader is for the writer to find some aspect of the subject that interests or excites him. This search for an interesting angle may provide just what is needed in the way of self-involvement.

Making use of the typewriter. One final comment regarding the preparation of themes and papers is in order here. A typed paper is likely to command more attention and respect from an instructor than one that is handwritten, no matter how neat the writing is. In these days of steadily escalating college enrollments, instructors find that they have less and less time to read the work of more and more students. Having to struggle through handwritten papers merely adds to the frustration and tension they are already experiencing. Indeed, many instructors are demanding that all papers be typed and are refusing to read those that are handwritten.

Even when typing is not required, the student has nothing to lose and may have a great deal to gain by typing his paper or having it typed, since there is a tendency (probably unconscious) for instructors to rate typed papers higher than handwritten ones, particularly if the handwriting is something less than perfect.

Empathy helps here, also, as it does in all matters of communication between student and instructor. The student who anticipates the instructor's reaction to his paper will type it to make sure that his message is as clear and unambiguous as possible. To use the term I introduced a few paragraphs back, turning in a handwritten paper introduces "noise" into the communication channel, and the more "noise," the less understanding.

Students often object to the requirement that papers be typed, pointing out that they have never learned to type, do not have a typewriter, or cannot afford the expense. Students who understand the need to reduce "noise" in the communication channels between them and their instructors are unlikely to raise such objections. Students who have never typed will find, for example, that after a little practice they can type with two fingers—"hunt and peck"— as fast as they can write by hand. They also find, to their surprise, that typing enables them to spot errors more readily than they can with handwriting. With respect to objections to the cost, the question resolves itself to a matter of priorities. The serious student regards the purchase of a portable typewriter in the same light as the purchase of a dictionary or a thesaurus: a necessary and unavoidable educational expense. Many college libraries provide rental typewriters for student use at a low fee—ten cents for a half hour is a common rate. The person who owns a typewriter, however, is more likely to make use of it. For those students who are unable to type, the purchase of a typewriter also enhances the possibility that they will learn to use it.

One more practical note: students should always make carbon copies—for insurance, if for no other reason, because instructors occasionally lose or misplace papers. Since carbon copies can be made more efficiently by typewriter, this is still another argument in favor of typing papers.

Class discussion. An increasing number of instructors today make use of class discussion as a major instructional technique. This trend is particularly noticeable in classes in the behavioral sciences and in the humanities, but the technique is used in other fields as well. Discussion may take the form of what is termed "free discussion," with the instructor playing a minor part, or may be of the more traditional type, with the instructor taking a more directive role. Some instructors favor some form of "Socratic method," whereby they attempt, through a series of questions, to get students to think through problems and to take the initiative in discovering concepts and interrelationships among events.

A common complaint that students make about class discussions is that they have to listen to a few individuals do all the talking. Listening to other students talk can be a tedious experience, but the tedium can be easily avoided. The cure for this problem is participation. Easier said than done, of course, because students who are used to carrying the burden of class discussion have developed the knack of knowing when one can break in, when to start and when to stop speaking. It is only by risking a few awkward interruptions, however, that one learns how to discuss. Like other skills of learning I have discussed, the mere practice of this technique changes one's motivation: one begins to listen differently, the concepts being discussed take on new meaning, and the whole instructional form becomes more interesting. Students who resist entering discussions because they have nothing to say can begin their involvement with a question. It is easier to pose a question than to make a statement. After a few sessions of raising questions, one becomes more at ease and is ready for the next step: making a statement.

FEEDBACK

It is impossible to learn anything of importance without making mistakes. We cannot learn to skate unless we fall down a few times, because it is through falling that we learn how to keep our balance and to avoid falls.

Feedback consists of information indicating what effects our behavior has had on the environment. Feedback, as it applies to learning, relates to information regarding the degree to which our attempts at learning have succeeded or failed. The grades we receive on papers and quizzes are a form of feedback because they inform us of the relative effectiveness of our performance in the eyes of the instructor or reader. In group discussion, the reaction of others to our comments provides us with clues as to whether our attempts at communication have been successful or whether our contributions and suggestions have been received and accepted. All human interaction involves some form of valuing, conscious or otherwise. It is difficult to react to any human action—our own or another's—without making some kind of comparison with the behavior of others, with our expectations, and the like. Such comparisons are also made relative to some obvious or implied standard. Let us say that we have volunteered for a committee to redraft the constitution and by-laws of the Associated Students. As we meet with the committee for the first time, each member is making judgments about the other members both in terms of what he expects of himself and what he hopes and expects others will contribute. And so it is with a countless number of social situations. Whenever we interact with others, we watch for clues that will reveal how they judge us, just as they watch us for similar clues.

Instructors play a special role with respect to feedback.

Whereas other people provide feedback information informally or incidentally, it is the responsibility of each instructor to tell his students how effective their performance has been in terms of the standards he has set for the course. Although such evaluation can be anxiety-provoking, it is nonetheless a valuable part of the learning experience. A considerable number of research studies show that we can do a much better job of learning if we are given information on how well we are doing, since feedback shows up our errors, enables us to identify weaknesses that need correcting, and makes the whole learning process more interesting.

Feedback, as we have noted, tells us how others are evaluating us. The process is more formalized and hence more obvious in the interaction that takes place in the college classroom than in most social situations. We have noted how feedback can occur as a result of our completion of assignments. Tests, quizzes, and examinations are also designed to provide feedback. The "anxiety potential" of tests is so high that few students recognize that they provide a major opportunity to communicate with the instructor. An examination question is, in effect, a demand on the part of the instructor that the student tell him what he knows about the topic in question. Test items usually are relatively restrictive, to be sure, and the student consequently does not have full freedom to tell *all* he knows. On the other hand, the student does not have sufficient time to tell all he has learned during the course, either, nor does the instructor have enough time to evaluate all that the student could tell him. The instructor therefore frames a question that will enable him to *sample* the student's knowledge.

The instructor has the task of trying to find questions that will not only give students a chance to say what they know on a subject but that will also enable him to make the kinds of interstudent comparisons that are necessary in evaluation. If a question is too general, he may get so many different kinds of answers that it is not possible to compare one student with another. By limiting the range of possible answers he is able to have some basis for such comparisons. Students often object to the limitations placed on them by the questions posed by the instructor because they would prefer to discuss aspects of the subject that are more familiar to them. One interesting reaction to this difference between what the instructor has asked and what students want to tell him appears in a rather common tendency for students to distort or misinterpret the question in ways that enable them to write on topics with which they feel more comfortable. A student who is asked, "What economic factors led up to the War of 1812?" might feel more at home describing the *political* events leading up to that war and will somehow conclude that such an answer would be acceptable. His decision is probably an unconscious one; at least, most students who make such "reinterpretations" of a question seem surprised to learn that their instructors find their answers inappropriate.

In order to do an adequate job of answering examination questions, students must recognize that the usual rules of interpersonal communication apply here, just as they do in oral exchanges. As I pointed out in the section on writing papers, the students must develop some idea of the instructor's intentions, otherwise they will have no idea why he has asked such a question. Students who have used their classroom interaction with the instructor as a way of determining his interests, values, attitudes, and teaching style are in a good position to initiate the kinds of response that will enable the instructor to do a decent job of evaluation and feedback. The student who identifies with the instructor and who has taken on some of his values, at least tentatively, is in the best position of all. Such a student is often able to anticipate the kinds of questions the instructor will ask, as well as the kinds of answers he expects.

The student who is preoccupied with his own needs or who rejects the instructor's values out of hand has, in effect, introduced "noise" in the communication channel between himself and the instructor. He is more easily distracted from the message contained in the examination question and is more likely to introduce distortions and misinterpretations.

I have made a particular point about the importance of empathy in both communication and learning. It is impossible to develop any kind of empathic relationship with another person without getting some kind of feedback. Without feedback, we are unable to gauge how the other person will respond to our attempts to communicate with him. Although test-taking and other forms of evaluation are what psychologists call "stress situations," students can use them effectively to learn something about the instructor—not merely a particular instructor, but instructors in general. Much of what students know about instructors by the time they enter college has been gained from the evaluation that has been made of their work by teachers 'in elementary and secondary schools, and one of the reasons why they are not more empathic, where instructors are concerned, is their reluctance to use the information they have. Still another reason, of course, is the general lack of awareness of the importance of empathy in the educational process.

The successful student, on the other hand, is one who recognizes that getting an education is essentially a communicative process, and that successful communication cannot take place unless there is personal involvement at both ends—involvement on the part of the recipient of messages as well as on the part of the initiator. Empathy facilitates involvement, because it alerts initiators and recipients of messages to problems of meaning. The initiator becomes concerned with the way in which his messages are being interpreted, and the receiver, with determining the intentions of the messages' initiator.

CHAPTER SIX

Getting the most out
of instructors

WHAT can you do to make educational processes function more efficiently?

WHO is to blame when students don't learn?

CAN students and instructors really cooperate as partners?

How can you get along with an instructor without "selling out" to an authority figure?

How do students punish instructors who are trying to be effective?

ARE instructors really people, and how can you find out?

YOU have a problem, you make an appointment with an instructor, you face him alone in his office—then what?

SHOULD you apologize to an instructor about taking up his valuable time?

IN which roles are instructors more effective: as reinforcers or as models?

Is it too much to expect a student taking a single course in biology to become a part-time biologist?

WHAT can you do about "problem instructors?"

SHOULD instructors grade according to the amount of work a student has done?

MAKING THE EDUCATIONAL PROCESS
MORE EFFECTIVE

IN the foregoing chapters, I have emphasized the need for students to involve themselves in the educational process if they are to derive any enduring benefits from the college years. The arguments I gave in this respect were based on the premise that learning has meaning only to the extent that learners are personally involved in and committed to what they are doing. In my discussions of this issue, I have concentrated on the student and the material he is to learn. Therefore, I may, at times, have presented a picture of the student alone in the educational world valiantly coping with a mountain of problems. Although much of the student's work *is* done alone, he is in fact a member of a college community and interacts with students, faculty, and staff every day. Thus he is surrounded by a large number of individuals who are potential sources of help in his struggle to get an education and to keep his head above water, academically speaking. In this chapter, I shall discuss how a student might make use of his instructors and, in the following chapter, how he might make use of other students.

One of the reasons why a student needs help is that educational processes are never as efficient or as effective as they are supposed to be. There is nothing especially startling about this observation, because no process that involves human beings can be expected to function at absolute, top theoretical efficiency. There is always some slippage, some wastage. Attempts to communicate may fail because participants, unbeknownst to one another, work at cross purposes and inadvertently sabotage their own efforts. Efficiency is, however, a relative matter. Processes can be *more* or *less* efficient, and, as long as we are participants in a process, we have within our hands the power to enhance or reduce its efficiency.

In spite of the fact that these social processes, such as communication, are much less efficient than we would like them to be, we nevertheless cannot function without them. Furthermore, we can take some comfort in the fact that they work efficiently enough to do the job most of the time. Face-to-face communication and cooperation, however, enjoy a built-in advantage that is lacking in much education—that of prompt feedback. A person who has said the wrong thing usually gets some kind of immediate reaction from his listeners, a reaction that enables him to make adjustments in the messages he is emitting in order to increase the sensitivity of his audience to his messages and to make them clearer.

Education, on the other hand, belongs to a class of social processes that have long-range effects. We can tell that education is effective because measurable changes take place in students over a period of years, and people who have had the benefit of more education tend to differ in a number of ways from those who have had less. But the student seldom gets the kind of immediate feedback in educational activities that he is likely to experience in a conversation or when he is working on a complex task with a group of collaborators. This lack of immediate feedback not only makes it difficult for students to make adjustments in their approach to a task but also deprives them of an important source of satisfaction. In other words, feedback has a reinforcing effect where learning is concerned. Getting approving responses from others while learning leads us to repeat what we are doing and to continue along the same general lines. Such an experience is reassuring and rewarding. In most educational tasks, however, feedback is postponed for long periods of time. The paper that is handed in on Monday may not be returned until the following week. Delays of a week or two between taking an examination and getting it back graded are common. And a great deal of what a student does evokes no reaction at all from the instructor, who is concerned with responding to the mass behavior of a class of twenty, thirty, or a hundred students and is in no position to reinforce much of anything. In many courses, feedback may not take place until the term reports appear, weeks or months after the course is over.

One reason why I have stressed that success in learning depends on the active involvement of the learner is that students tend to place the responsibility for successful or unsuccessful learning experiences on the shoulders of the instructor. There is some validity in this practice because instructors are in strategic positions to stimulate or impede learning. However, this fact does not diminish the validity of the argument that the *prime* responsibility for learning (or not learning) is that of the student. Some instructors are more successful than others at stimulating students to learn. Therefore, an additional reason why educational processes are inefficient may be found in the great variability in the skills of instructors. This may be resented, but it should not be a cause for despair, not as long as students are willing to take a major degree of responsibility for their own learning.

Not all of the instructor behavior to which students are exposed is directly concerned with education. Some of it is in the nature of academic ritual, some meets the instructor's needs for self-expression, and some raises a kind of psychological barrier between instructor and student. It is simple to say that instructors should not do anything that does not aid or facilitate learning, but that is easier said than done. Some of this nonfunctional behavior results from instructors' own needs for self-expression, and some of it is a by-product of their attempts to clarify their own roles with respect to students. Students, for their part, also engage in forms of behavior that are nonfunctional with respect to learning, that are concerned with personal needs for self-expression, and that are concerned with maintaining social distance between themselves and their instructors as well as between themselves and other students. Although some of this behavior may interfere with learning, most of it actually maintains a degree of psychological comfort in a social situation. If the social distance between instructor and student were, for example, reduced to its absolute minimum, both would feel quite uncomfortable and would look for some way in which to end or escape from the relationship.

Still another factor that reduces the efficiency of educational processes is the fact that they must take place within the context of what is usually a fairly large group. Colleges and universities do not generally have the time, money, facilities, or personnel to conduct education on a person-to-person, tutorial basis. Curricula, textbooks, teaching aids, and teaching methods are all selected by instructors with principles of mass education in mind. Decisions are made primarily in terms of what will help the *mass* of students learn. The presence of a number of students may also present some advantages but, for the moment, we shall consider the need to conduct education on a mass basis as still another factor that reduces its efficiency, as far as the needs of individual students are concerned.

HOW STUDENTS MAY MAKE EDUCATIONAL PROCESSES MORE EFFICIENT

Students and instructors are partners in an educational venture. This does not mean that the partnership is necessarily an equal one, because instructors generally have higher status, more prestige, and what is usually a greater degree of expertness. But it does mean that learning is not likely to occur unless instructors and students work together in some kind of collaborative fashion. The instructor generally has the initiative in determining what procedures are to be followed and what standards are to be met, but the student is not without power. Undoubtedly, he can undermine the entire operation by going through the motions of doing what the instructor requires and, at the same time, refusing to learn anything that can be retained beyond the final examination. Sometimes the social climate of an entire class or even an entire school is oriented toward this type of subtle sabotage.

The student can therefore facilitate the success of the educational process by recognizing that he has roles to play that are more than merely passive and by finding ways to play them. He can recognize that there are deficiencies in the educational process and try to find ways to make it work better. This may sound like "selling out," to those who are more than usually troubled by "authority problems," but it is an approach that will make the student's participation more interesting and rewarding.

We begin with the matter of immediate feedback. Students who are willing to move closer to instructors—for instance, by approaching them before or after class or during office hours— are in a better position to get immediate feedback on questions and ideas. Most instructors are willing to engage in a discussion of the material covered by the course and may even be flattered that anyone cares enough to ask questions. But there are times when contact with the instructor is not possible, and only section leaders, readers, or student assistants are available. In this event, these individuals should be approached on the grounds that some feedback is better than no feedback. A student should be sure, however, that the instructor actually is unavailable. Students (and student assistants as well) sometimes create a myth that an instructor is not interested in students and does not want to be bothered by them. But the truth is that the instructor is perfectly willing to talk to them as long as they are seriously interested in his fields of interest.

The problem of what to do about an instructor whose teaching methods leave something to be desired is a perplexing one. One group of students in a calculus course organized their own study section outside of class and were able to keep up with assignments quite adequately. This solution requires considerable leadership and self-discipline on the part of students, but it does show that there are ways to deal with difficult situations.

Another approach is that of using reinforcement. No matter how unskilled the instructor, he is bound to have some class sessions that run better than others. It is quite proper for students to tell him on these occasions that the class was interesting or that it seemed especially helpful. It is also legitimate for them to remind him of his more successful classes: "When are we going to do role playing again?" (Foreign languages) "Is there any chance that you will be talking on little-known edible plants again?" (Botany) "We were all interested when you talked about the historical background of classic experiments. Could we have some more of this sometime?" (Physics; chemistry)

When instructors try to modify their approaches, students often miss opportunities to help them use more effective methods. The lecturer finishes his assigned quota for the day and then says: "We have a few minutes left for questions. Are there any?" The class waits with bated breath because they may get out ten minutes early if no questions are asked. This refusal to ask questions may punish the instructor for having delivered such a dull lecture, but it also discourages him from opening the class hour for dialogue. It may also reinforce his "stereotype" of students and "prove" that they are all intellectually lazy.

Students also punish the instructor who ends a lecture with "Are there any questions?" by asking questions that are completely irrelevant to the material he has presented. For example, "What chapters will Tuesday's quiz cover?" A question of this type says to the instructor "We are not interested in, do not care about, or do not understand what you have been talking about. Let's get on to something that really concerns us, namely, what you are going to ask us in the next quiz." Instructors are more impressionable than is generally known. One study showed that high school teachers tended to modify their approach to teaching when they were told what students thought of the methods they were using (Gage, Runkel, and Chatterjee, 1960). It appears that students are not as powerless in their relationships with faculty as they might think.

To be absolutely realistic about students' chances for getting instructors to improve, I must admit that there are instances in which students can have little or any effect on instructor behavior. This is likely to occur, for example, in large lecture classes where the very size of the group prevents much contact between instructor and student. Some instructors who teach small classes, too, have through the years learned some very effective ways of insulating themselves from student communication. It would be self-defeating for students in classes like these to stop learning. In situations of this sort, students may actually be freer agents than the instructor: after all, he has become frozen in a pattern of behavior which he cannot change and from which he cannot escape, whereas they are able to change and can modify *their* behavior to meet the situation.

GETTING TO KNOW INSTRUCTORS AS PEOPLE

Students often complain that an instructor does not know them as individuals. He does not recognize them outside of class; in class, he does not remember names, or matches the wrong names with wrong faces; he does not seem to care how hard students work and how much time they have put into his course; and so on. A fair counterargument to these complaints is: "How well do the students know the instructor as an individual?"

This is a reasonable question for a number of reasons. First, it points up the one-sidedness of the complaints: the students are saying, in effect, that it is more important for the instructor to recognize them as individuals than it is for them to recognize him as an individual. Second, students are in a much better position to get to know the instructor than he is to become acquainted with them. He is only one person; they are fifteen, thirty, or whatever number there are in the class. It is obviously easier to get to know one person as an individual than to get to know fifteen, thirty, or one hundred. Information regarding instructors is also readily available. Most college catalogs list the schools, academic preparation of their faculty members, and many instructors are listed in *Who's who* (regional or national), directories of professional societies, or *American men of science*. College catalogs or time schedules often list other courses an instructor teaches, and these provide additional clues as to his interests. If the instructor has published, it should not be too difficult to glance over what he has written. Publications, if any, are probably the best single source

90

of information regarding an instructor's interests, and his attitudes and values as well. Even a brief examination of these background data will give the student a new and better perspective on what is going on in the course.

I have already commented on the desirability of meeting the instructor face to face before or after class or in his office. Any item of interest common to both student and instructor may be discussed at these times. Students are likely to be anxious and concerned about grades, examinations, requirements and standards for assigned work, but such matters should be relegated to second place and, most desirably, should not be discussed at all unless the instructor chooses to bring them up. A face-to-face encounter is an opportunity for both instructor and student to get to know each other as persons, and interpersonal understanding cannot occur unless a topic of genuine interest to both is discussed. Instructors generally are not very interested in the evaluational and other technical aspects of their teaching, but they *are* likely to be interested in the subject they teach.

Students might prepare for such an encounter by looking over the materials the instructor has provided for the course—reading lists, course outlines, or whatever—for clues that will indicate the kind of professional interests the instructor has. It certainly is advisable to look at any books he has recommended. The task here is that of taking the instructor *seriously*—just as seriously as you want him to take you. The instructor may have casually mentioned a reference as worth reading. His offhand manner may indicate that he does not think the reference is very important, but actually he would not have mentioned it if he did not think it had some merit. Students are bound to gain by following up on these clues, and instructors are invariably pleased to learn that someone has followed one of their suggestions.

Topics to discuss with instructors are not as difficult to find as we might think. All you need is a few leads. Relevance is one. Almost every specialty has some relevance to the everyday life of the student. Is there any relationship, for example, between what you are studying in chemistry and air and water pollution? The question you ask should show that you have thought about the matter and have tried to make some kind of interpretation or to find some relationship. There is nothing wrong with making an incorrect interpretation; most instructors take pleasure in showing students where they have made incorrect deductions or have foundered on faulty logic.

For students who are contemplating a change of major, instructors are excellent sources of information about the courses and fields of concentration that are required or are available in their fields, what kind of work a graduate in the major may enter, and what the job prospects are. Even a marginal concern about the field as a possible major is a legitimate reason for inquiries along these lines.

Students are often apologetic about taking up an instructor's time. It *is* appropriate to ask whether he has time to answer a few questions about the course or his specialty, but it is not necessary to apologize for one's presumptiousness in taking him away from important tasks. Various conditions operate to create a psychological and social gulf between instructors and students that is already too great and that interferes with easy and effective communication. When students attempt to demean themselves by effusive apologies or other tactics that exaggerate social distance, they worsen the relationship and make mutual understanding even more difficult. The best approach is a simple and natural one. Under most conditions, it is reasonable for students to assume that they have a right to a modest portion of an instructor's time. If the instructor says that he is busy with something that cannot be interrupted, it is legitimate to ask when a more convenient time would be and to set up an appointment. Generally, it is a good idea to make appointments rather than to drop in unannounced during the instructor's office hours. It is not so much that the unscheduled interview is bad form, for instructors have office hours at least partly for the purpose of making themselves available to students. But appointments are advisable, because the student who drops in may find that the instructor is already talking to someone, and others may be waiting. Having an appointment gives one a certain priority. The priority is not necessarily ironclad; instructors are often called out of their offices unexpectedly by unforseen problems. Teaching and meeting with students are not the only responsibilities of instructors. They are also involved with the organizational aspects of the college and must participate in committees, departmental meetings, and conferences, which are sometimes called with very little advance notice. Hence a student who has been "stood up" by an instructor should not take it personally, but should make at least one more try.

Seeking out and talking to instructors does call for a bit of courage, persistence, and poise, and the student who is shy or retiring may decide that the cost in terms of possible rejection or embarrassment is greater than the possible gain. It is probably trite to say that this is the kind of student who has the most to gain from talking to his instructors. A realization that these interviews are important is not likely to make it easier for the timid student to take himself in hand and force himself to initiate a contact. What such students can do, however, is to conduct their interviews in pairs. Some individuals find it easier to interact with persons in authority (like instructors) if they have the support of another person. Teaming up with a partner on an assignment like this also has the advantage of developing a working relationship with another student that could be used to some profit on other types of learning tasks.

THE INSTRUCTOR AS A MODEL AND A REINFORCER OF LEARNING

Like it or not, the instructor has considerable control over what a student learns and how much he learns. This is the chief reason for getting to know him as a person. If the class is exciting and interesting, it is worth getting to know the instructor in order to enlarge on the learning that is taking place. If the class is boring and dull, the student has nothing to lose and may have much to gain by becoming better acquainted with the instructor. In this instance, the behavior of the instructor is serving to impede or discourage learning, and the student needs to get some new perspectives on the relationship between him and the instructor in order to derive some benefit from the time and energy he is already putting into the course.

Instructors are able to affect the kind of learning that goes on in their classroom partly because they are able to reinforce certain kinds of behaviors—that is, the power they have to award grades, to comment orally or in writing on the statements students make, and to encourage or discourage puts them in a position to facilitate or to interfere with learning processes. One problem that tends to reduce this power, however, is the one that we mentioned previousiy: the long delay between the point at which the student makes a response in the form of a completed assignment or an examination and the point at which he receives reinforcement. A second problem, also mentioned previously, relates to the mass nature of most college education: a single instructor must spread whatever reinforcement he has to make over several dozen students. The total impact of instructor reinforcement on a single student therefore may, be somewhat diluted in its effect. We have noted, in the foregoing section, how students can, through personal interviews with an instructor, receive more reinforcement than they would ordinarily experience, but the number of students who can take advantage of this opportunity is likely to be limited. An instructor obviously cannot interact individually with every student once or twice a week.

The power of the instructor as a reinforcer of learning is, therefore, fairly diffuse. If reinforcement enters into college learning to any great extent, it is because students have somehow discovered how to find their own satisfactions in learning and have thus become their own reinforcers.

There are other kinds of contributions that instructors make to classroom situations that have a more important effect on students' learning. One such contribution appears in the form of the kinds of attitudes that students develop toward the subject being taught. Students learn in a course partly because the instructor *expects* them to learn. The fact that he thinks his subject is important enough to study and that it can be learned by students gets them off to an optimistic start in their work. They may have doubts (many of them) about their ability to complete the work and pass the instructor's examinations, but the fact that he appears before them every class period, a living symbol of the college's expectation that they will succeed, is a source of encouragement to them. It is true that much that instructors do also *dis*courages students but, for the moment, we are concerned about what they do that encourages them and hence facilitates learning.

The instructor also influences learning in another subtle way: he represents a kind of a model to students. Every academic field has its special set of attitudes, values, and behaviors. This fact is the basis of the qualities that make people in fields like history, chemistry, and philosophy different from one another. If you were to visit the faculty dining room at noon, you would find that instructors from the same academic departments are more likely to eat together than with faculty from other departments. They do this because they have more in common with people from their own specialties and find it easier to communicate with them. The more that viewpoints, problems, and special vocabularies are shared, the more comfortable people are with one another.

What I am saying is that there are qualities that people in a given specialty have in common and that distinguish them from people in other specialties. Indeed, one of the things that students learn during their stay in college is how people in various specialties differ from one another, but this is not our major concern here. A biology instructor, if he is successful, will also get his students to act, think, and behave like biologists, at least for the time that they are studying biology. Every biology student, therefore, is expected to become a part-time biologist. He is expected to be interested in the kind of phenomena that interest biologists and to perceive and understand them as biologists do. This will require, of course, that he will have at his command a fund of the kind of information that biologists possess and will use the terminology, concepts, and techniques that biologists use. In other words, what biology students learn is to play some of the roles and adopt some of the perspectives that are peculiar to biologists.

Their model in this respect is their instructor. It is through copying his behavior that they learn the appropriate roles and perspectives, and his evaluation of their progress will be in terms of the extent to which they have been able to take on biologists' roles and perspectives.

Students who are more successful are aware of this need to use the instructor as a model in learning the values, attitudes, and roles he displays, although most of them would probably be unable to describe it in the terms I have used. Students who are less successful tend to resist the efforts of the instructor to get them to think along the lines used by people in his specialty or else are completely unaware of the importance of doing so. To put this into other terms that we have used previously, the more successful students are able to *identify* with the instructor and use him as a model for their behavior, whereas the less successful students isolate themselves from him. To his request that they adopt the language, concepts, and attitudes of his specialty, they reply, in effect: "Just tell us what we have to do to pass the course (or get a high mark) and we'll do it." Such a reaction is a rejection of the instructor and a denial both of the validity of his subject, as well as of the need to develop new perspectives in order to accomplish real learning.

I want to make it clear that the role-playing undertaken by successful students must be done on a part-time basis. A student who takes five courses a term will have five instructor-models, and each one may be in a different specialty. This complicates life, but it does not present an impossible task. Students can learn to be flexible, to play the role of the mathematician, the psychologist, the literary critic, and the artist—and all in the same morning.

College students are certainly not inexperienced in using others as models for their attitudes and behavior. Much of what we are today is the result of such learning. We started using parents as models during early childhood. By the time we began to attend school we were already using other adults and older children as models. Many of our beliefs and values were learned not so much because we were *told* what to believe but because they were a part of the personality and behavior of people we admired, with whom we identified, and who we used as models for our behavior.

This is one of the reasons why it is important to develop some understanding of the instructor as a person. The better we know a person, the better we understand his values and attitudes, and the more able we are to use him as a model.

The instructor who is not liked does present a special problem. In this instance we should remind ourselves that we are not using the *whole* individual as our model—only those aspects of his behavior that relate to his specialty. Part of our task, therefore, will be that of determining what the significant aspects are that can be used in the new role we are learning.

Garrison has a number of suggestions on ways in which students can cope with "problem instructors." Here they are, in somewhat modified form:

Don't waste energy resenting a boring lecture; instead, try to do a better job of stating in your own mind what the instructor is trying to say.

If the instructor has annoying habits, try to forget him as a person for the moment and concentrate on the meaning of the concepts and facts he is presenting.

If something is said that you don't understand, frame a question on the point as clearly and as precisely as you can and jot it down in your notes. It may be possible to raise the question with the instructor during a discussion period or after class or to look it up later in the library.

Do not evaluate too hastily. It may be that the major difficulty is the all-too-common tendency to base our judgments of others on first impressions that are categorized into good-bad, like-dislike.

If ideas are presented that you dislike or resent, ask yourself *why* the instructor presents these ideas. What is he getting at? What is his frame of reference?

Be on guard against closing your mind when you hear words or expressions about which you have strong feelings or biases. For instance, if an instructor says, "Religion has no place in scientific investigations," try to determine *why* he made the statement and don't just tell yourself, "He's wrong there," or "He's an atheist."

Above all, try to understand the frame of reference—the *why*—of the instructor. You may come to like him or you may not, but in any event the experience of being in his class will be worthwhile. And if you say afterwards, "I learned English history in spite of Dr. Smith, not because of him," take satisfaction in the fact that you *did* learn something from having been in the class.

THE INSTRUCTOR AS AN AUTHORITY FIGURE

Effect of earlier experiences with teachers. All our lives we have had to deal with persons who possess power and authority and hence are in a position to influence or control our behavior—*authority figures,* to use the psychologist's term. These earlier experiences are not readily outgrown: whatever attitudes we developed toward persons in authority during childhood and adolescence are likely to appear in some form in our relations with college instructors. This does not mean that our attitudes toward college instructors are going to be exactly like those we had toward high school and elementary school teachers, but it does mean that attitudes toward instructors—particularly the impressions on our initial encounter—will be colored by our earlier experiences. The student who tended to be hostile and resistive toward his teachers in high school will try to test the authority of instructors in college. The student whose strategy in high school was that of sticking closely to the instructor's requirements (which are usually specified more exactly in high school than they are in college) may encounter difficulty in determining what it is that college instructors expect of him. The student who developed a close personal relationship with favorite instructors in high school may have difficulty in finding many college instructors that are willing to permit such an arrangement.

High school teachers and college instructors. Many of the approaches that students use successfully in high school will also work in college. Like high school teachers, college teachers respond favorably to neatness, promptness, respect, enthusiasm, and all the other qualities that evoke favorable reactions from high school teachers. College instructors are, after all, teachers, and tasks of teaching and learning are quite similar in both educational contexts. We would be less than realistic, however, if we did not recognize some rather significant differences between the two groups of teachers. College instructors are, as a group, more interested and involved in their specialty than high school teachers, and also are less likely to be personally interested in students. These differences are relative and not absolute. There are many dedicated scholars in high school, and many warm, sympathetic college instructors who are willing and even eager to play accepting and supportive roles as advisers and counselors for students. But the differences between high school and college teachers are there for anyone who wants to notice them, just as there are differences in the psychological climate or atmosphere between high school and college.

Teachers are not parents. The first authority figures we experience are our parents, and these early experiences tend to color our relations with authority figures all our lives. One of the problems of growing up and becoming mature is that of realizing that teachers and other authority figures are *not* our parents, even though they might behave in parentlike ways on occasion—admonishing, chiding, punishing, and rewarding. As we go through school, the parental roles of teachers become less and less important, just as the other roles they play become more important. By the time students reach college, relatively little remains of the parent in most of the instructors. This can be difficult for the student who has not awakened to this fact and who persists in ascribing parental qualities to college instructors. He may expect, for example, that they will remind him of papers that have not been turned in on time. The fact is that most college instructors assume that the student has made the decision not to turn in a paper freely and has, in effect, chosen to take a failing grade. Decisions like these are the student's to make, without interference or nagging from the instructor.

Rewards for work accomplished. Another misconception that students bring with them from high school is the idea that the sheer amount of work a student does should have some kind of a reward. Writing a good paper usually does take a good deal of work, but many students work very hard and are still unable to produce papers that come up to a reasonable standard. This is likely to happen when students have been unable to grasp the frame of reference used by the instructor and are, instead, merely trying to meet the specific course requirements. They are naturally disappointed when the instructor does not take the amount of work into account when he assigns his grade, but marks instead on other factors, such as the level of thinking that he believes is revealed by the paper.

Another example is the student who realizes that he is receiving grades that are less than satisfactory and who asks the instructor if he can do any extra work in order to raise his grade. The instructor replies that the student can do extra work if he wishes, but that the final grade will be based on the instructor's opinion of the level of competence the student has developed in dealing with the material covered by the course. In both instances, the student seems to believe that the purpose of education is to get students to work—to suffer, if you like—and that the more work (and the more the suffering), the higher the grade. Although it is true that a few college instructors do follow the secondary school practice of grading according to the amount of time and energy a student has expended, most of them are more likely to be impressed by his command of the subject, the level at which he is functioning, and the like.

It may be that I have painted a less sympathetic portrait of college instructors in this section than I intended and hence have discouraged some readers from becoming better acquainted with them. If so, such was not my purpose, because I believe that communication between student and instructor will improve if both draw psychologically closer, the one to the other. The distance that usually separates them leads to misperception and misunderstanding. Students ought to get to know instructors as people, just as instructors should get to know students as people.

The main point in this section, however, is that students should be aware of the differences between college instructors and other teachers they have known. It is not so much that college instructors are less interested in students than grade school and high school teachers are, but rather that they are considerably more interested in ideas. And they are first and foremost subject-matter specialists. A high school teacher of biology holds his job principally because he is a teacher, whereas an instructor of biology in college has been hired because he is a biologist.

College students have known teachers most of their lives, but attending college gives them a chance to get to know people who are not only teachers but who have also established themselves as scholars, scientists, or specialists in a particular field of competence.

CHAPTER SEVEN

Learning and other students

WHY is it that instructors and students so often work at cross-purposes?

"THE student is in a marginal position." Is this an advantage or a disadvantage? What should he do about this situation?

WHY are some students afraid of instructors who are really effective?

How are parents likely to feel about the way in which colleges change students?

How can you use your membership in clubs and other voluntary organizations to help you become more successful academically?

WHY is the cost of hiring a tutor likely to be a sound investment and a bargain?

UNDER what conditions should students making average grades serve as tutors?

IF studying is a lonely business, what is the value of having a partner?

WHAT disadvantages are there in studying with others?

Learning and the environment. Learning is the result of our interaction with our environment. As we react to various aspects of this interaction, we make changes and modifications in our responses. Some of these responses become stabilized and show up as relatively permanent features of our general behavior.

The fact that the college environment has certain characteristics possessed by no other type of environment means that individuals who interact with it will develop the qualities and behavior patterns that we have come to associate with an educated person. One explanation of the changes that take place in a given student during the college years may be found in the nature of the environment to which he is responding. Another explanation may be found in the way in which he initiates and sustains interaction with the environment.

When I use the term "environment" in this context, I refer to more than the physical aspects of the college campus. These aspects are, for the most part, passive and inert, like the books in the library and the physical arrangement of classrooms and buildings. The more significant aspects of the college environment are active, and in this connection I have in mind the individuals and groups with whom the student associates. It is his association with these people that plays a significant role in the attitudes, values, and patterns of behavior he learns. In other words, they make an important contribution to the person he is becoming.

In the previous chapter I discussed the various ways in which students interact with instructors. Many people believe that the instructor-student relationship is the only significant one in the educational process, but behavioral scientists who have studied the college scene have turned up considerable evidence which shows that the relationships among and between students also exert a considerable degree of influence on the learning that takes place during the college years. In the preceding chapter we noticed that instructors can stimulate learning because they can reinforce certain aspects of student behavior and also because they may serve as models who may be imitated. Students also may influence one another along the same lines: by reinforcing behavior and by serving as models.

HOW STUDENTS CAN INTERFERE WITH NORMAL LEARNING PROCESSES

Conflicts between student goals and instructor goals. Since what a student learns can be influenced both by his instructors and his fellow students, it follows that the best results will be obtained when the two sources of influence supplement and support one another. What often happens, however, is that they work at cross-purposes with each other. Whereas instructors generally try to influence the student to become more deeply involved in academic interests, his fellow students may influence him to reject instructional goals and, instead, to become involved in activities that are largely non-intellectual in nature.

We noted that the college environment is not like any other environment. It is unique largely because its leading sources of influence—instructors—are concerned with a form of behavior—the pursuit of ideas—that sets them apart from people in other walks of life. Not only do instructors engage in this rather unconventional form of behavior but they also develop a set of beliefs, attitudes, and values that are different from those of people outside of the college environment. Whereas instructors are a permanent part of the college environment (and to a large extent *are* the college environment), students occupy a kind of marginal position between the college and the world outside. For one thing, they are there only temporarily; for another, their past and future lies in the world outside the college. Many, indeed, maintain a dual existence and take part-time or full-time jobs during their stay in college.

This marginal position of the student means that he is more likely than his instructors to be exposed to the demands and pressures of the world outside the college. Hence it is understandable why he should be more easily distracted from tasks leading to involvement in academic matters. The world outside emphasizes the values of vocational success and getting along with others, whereas instructors are more likely to stress values of the scholar and scientist. The fact that the student is likely to be influenced by both the campus and the world outside inevitably creates conflicts for him. The research dealing with this problem shows that students have more to gain from their experience in college if they permit themselves to respond to college, rather than noncollege, sources of influence. The students who gain the most, for example, are those who are more interested in the pursuit of truth than in preparing themselves for a vocation although, as I shall point out in the next chapter, having a vocational objective is generally desirable. It resolves ambiguities about major fields and thus removes one source of distraction. Most students have vocational and academic objectives in mind, but there are some who focus exclusively on the vocational, just as there are those who become wholly committed to academic life. The vocationally oriented tend to specialize in fields that lead directly to careers, whereas the academic group tend to go into college teaching or research.

Differences in college campuses. Colleges differ in the extent to which their students respond to the two types of values: academic or nonacademic. On a few campuses, nonacademic values prevail, and instructors find it difficult to "get through to students." On these campuses, instructors can communicate with students as long as they confine themselves to everyday, nonacademic matters, but encounter difficulties when they try to get students concerned about academic goals. Students on such campuses present a fairly solid front against getting deeply involved in academic matters and attempt to get instructors to reduce their demands and make them as specific as possible so that they can be met by the minimum of involvement.

These conditions are more likely to be found on the campuses of colleges in which the student body is relatively homogeneous and is drawn from one social level or group or one geographical

106

area. The more students have in common, the easier it is for them to stand together in resisting the instructor's demands, thus blocking the instructor's hopes and expectations. They are also able to ridicule and bring other kinds of social pressure to bear in discouraging those students who would like to use instructors as models for their behavior. Such students who do cooperate with instructors are called "class-average raisers," or worse, and are sometimes subjected to teasing or ridicule in order to bring them into line.

Sanctions against serious students. Whenever individuals develop group solidarity, they are likely to develop consistent patterns of behavior called *norms*. The more the members of a group have in common with one another, the more closely knit the group is likely to be and the more important its norms become. If a sizeable number of students collectively develop attitudes and behavior patterns that enable them to resist the demands and expectations of their instructors, they have promulgated a norm for the group, and when individuals who are or should be members of the group behave in contrary fashion, it is natural that they should be subjected to some harassment and criticism. The solidarity of the group is threatened by the fact that some of their members are taking instructors seriously, whereas the other members have decided that instructors are to be obeyed in specific instances and to a limited degree (in order to remain in school and graduate), but are *not* to be taken seriously.

Reasons for student resistance to learning. There are a number of other reasons why students harass those who take learning seriously and want to involve themselves in academic matters. I have touched on a number of them in one way or another in this book. One is the conflict between needs to get along with the peer group —fellow students, for example—and needs to achieve and make progress intellectually. In Chapter Three we noted that students whose main concern is being accepted by their friends and acquaintances (social success) are less likely to be academically successful than are students who care less about social needs and more about moving ahead in the adult world. The latter type of students is inclined to be task-oriented, responsible, and responsive to the demands of persons in authority. The socially oriented individual has more difficulty in planning and carrying out the kind of strategies that succeed academically, partly because it goes against the grain for him to assign much importance to academic matters and partly because his continuing success in the social field is a built-in source of distractions for him. Furthermore, it is the socially successful person who provides the leadership on campuses where students combine to resist the demands and expectations of their instructors.

Students also resist learning because they find education a disturbing process. Students come to college with a kind of understanding of "the way things are," and their instructors offer them new ideas and perspectives that do not fit in with this view of the world and that are more or less upsetting. A great deal of the change in the individual that takes place as a result of his college experience comes as a result of his being upset and his attempts to find a kind of equilibrium. As David Riesman (1959) points out, the more successful the instructor, the more likely he is to disorient students. Some students find this process exciting, but others learn to be on their guard against instructors who are really effective in order to defend themselves against being disoriented and disturbed. Their defense may take the form of rejecting instructors' values and belittling their aims and objectives. The defensive stance may take the form of missing classes and not meeting deadlines for assigned papers. The strategies that have the most appeal to the resistive student, however, are the strategies that will enable him to obtain the socially valuable label of the bachelor's degree and at the same time help him to avoid the demands of the instructors.

Some students also find ways of interfering with or blocking learning processes because they are troubled by severe emotional problems, but what I have been describing above is a normal rather than a neurotic reaction toward situations that threaten to change one. Most of us do not like this or that quality about ourselves, but few of us want to undergo any major changes. Changes are painful and anxiety-provoking, and we would like to remain more or less the way we are, with our self-concept unchanged. Hence we can understand and even sympathize with the student who tries to evade or nullify the demands of college instructors. If we, as students, permit ourselves to become involved in the learning experiences they provide, change is inevitable, and the only way to prevent it is to resist learning. This is the strategy that is attempted by the less successful student. He may succeed so well in his approach, however, that he is dropped out of school as an academic failure. Or he may drop out spontaneously before failure occurs.

But what of the resistive individual who is able to remain in college until graduation—is he able to avoid change? In the first chapter I mentioned a study by Trent and Medsker (1968) which showed that college does tend to change students in rather fundamental ways, in the sense that students develop more intellectual interests, become more aware of themselves as individuals, and also develop a higher degree of autonomy (independence and the capacity for self-direction) than individuals who do not attend college. The study also showed that those who continued through the four years were more responsive to such changes than those who did not. It is very difficult for an individual to remain in an environment where changes are taking place in everyone, without being changed as well. Even internal changes have a way of being infectious. Some colleges bring about more changes in some students than others, of course, and the most change is likely to take place in colleges in which instructors are more scholarly and in which student bodies are made up of individuals from a wide variety of backgrounds.

Finally, I must mention that the changes that colleges induce in students may, at times, worsen relationships with parents. College campuses are inclined to permit a wide latitude of behavior —in dress, as in thought, for example—and parents who are already concerned about nonconformist tendencies on the part of their children are likely to think that colleges are encouraging them to go too far. Inasmuch as one source of liberating influence on the campus is faculty, some parents try to counteract instructor influence by aligning themselves with those students who are best able to resist academic influence.

HOW STUDENTS CAN FACILITATE NORMAL LEARNING PROCESSES

We noted in the foregoing section how student groups could insulate themselves, to some degree, against learning by developing· attitudinal and behavioral norms permitting conformity to instructors' demands in certain limited respects but enabling students to avoid real involvement with instructors' goals and interests. Student norms can also be of quite a different character, and may lead to a deeper involvement in the educational process. These norms are likely to develop spontaneously among students who come to college intending to major in special fields like art, business administration, music, engineering, and psychology—fields whose nature is well known outside the academic community. Student norms conducive to involvement are less likely to develop as spontaneously among students taking courses in the more traditional academic fields, although a particularly able instructor or group of instructors can get students quite excited about an area and, as a consequence, they may form a loyal, dedicated, and deeply involved group of followers.

Voluntary organizations of students. Interests in the various academic fields may also serve as a core for student organizations, and almost every student has a choice of belonging to Le Cercle Français, the Latin-American League, the Philosophical Forum, and so on. These organizations are composed, for the most part, of students with more-than-average commitment to the academic specialty represented.

There are several advantages that accrue to membership in such groups. If our behavior is shaped to a large extent by the people with whom we associate (and there is a great deal of research that indicates that it is, indeed, so), then it follows that students will improve their chances to learn and succeed by associating

110

with those who are already seriously involved in academic fields. We have noted previously that studying with another student on a special project, like preparing for an examination, can be very useful. We also noted that it is often difficult to find a partner who is willing to do this. A special interest group is a likely place to find such a person.

Still another advantage to membership in groups of this sort is that one gets to know the faculty members in the field, who often .act as sponsors of such groups. Getting to know these instructors can be very helpful when it comes to improving communication along the lines I have described in the last two chapters. Members of these groups are also useful sources of information about the field they represent. Through them, one can learn about recent trends and developments, what opportunities for further training and employment there are, scholarship information, and the like. These data are particularly useful for students who are exploring a number of possibilities with respect to selecting an academic major. There is no reason, of course, why a student who is considering several fields might not belong to more than one group.

Finding a study partner. The problem of finding a study partner, of course, may not be resolved by membership in a special interest club. A student who wants someone to work with in preparing for examinations in a given course generally does not have time to attend several weeks of meetings in the hope of finding a like-minded study partner. What he needs is someone to work with in preparing for next week's quiz. Locating a study partner can be a problem. We are usually reluctant to approach a strange student and ask whether he is interested in a cooperative arrangement on study, chiefly for fear of being rejected. Our chances for finding potential partners would be improved if we knew which ones would be more receptive to the offer. Here is one suggestion: If the instructor posts quiz grades, as many do, a student may be able to identify possible candidates by noting those who are making similar grades to his. This information makes it possible to go up to another student and say, "How did you feel about Friday's quiz? I see that we both got a C+, but I need to get better than

111

a C in this course. I've heard that studying with someone helps, and I need help! Would you like to try studying together for the next test?"

Another way of locating potential study partners is to observe who sits in the front rows during lecture periods. Students who are more serious about the course are likely to sit in this area partly because they do not want to miss anything and also because they wish to reduce the psychological distance between them and the instructor. Most of them are unaware of the latter motive, of course. Less committed and less successful students tend to sit as far back in the class as possible, partly because they hope that their inattention will not be noticed and partly because they want to maintain as much psychological distance as possible between them and the instructor. The best hunting for study partners will, therefore, be found in the first two or three rows.

Tutoring. If these tactics fail, there is still the possibility of hiring a tutor. Some colleges provide low-cost tutoring by honor students for those who are having academic difficulties, and this possibility should be investigated. In most colleges, however, the cost may run at least as high as the going rate for student help. The idea of paying two dollars or more an hour may seem like an outrageous proposal to students who are on a bare-bones budget, but the possibility should nevertheless be considered seriously. Tutoring can be very effective not only as a source of much needed instructional help but a motivator as well. A student who learns under the direction of a tutor is able to get immediate feedback and reinforcement, both valuable aids in facilitating learning. Working with a tutor also helps raise the interest level of the material and, as I pointed out in our chapter on communication, the fact that a tutor costs money is an extra incentive to do well and to find ways to eliminate his cost.

Another possibility is that of volunteering to help another student. Although you are making only average marks in a course, you may still be able to render valuable assistance to a student who is failing or is just on the borderline. The real gain for the tutor, however, lies in what *he* is able to learn through his efforts to

112

instruct. Anyone who has done any teaching knows that this is one of the best ways to learn a subject. When we explain a concept to another person we are enabled to see it more clearly and it becomes a more usable part of our fund of information. It is easier to repeat an idea on an examination or a term paper if we have previously put it into our own words. Tutoring another student can also make the subject more interesting and vital. When we play the role of tutor, we are also playing an instructional role and this should improve our own communicative relationship with the instructor. In other words, our tutoring enables us to see the material through the eyes of the instructor, and this in turn will give us an extra advantage when it comes to understanding his lectures and interpreting examination questions and assignments. Most students never gain this vantage point, because they are forever fixed in a "student" interpretation of the material and never realize that their viewpoint is quite different from an "instructor" perspective. Tutoring gives us a chance to develop a more flexible point of view regarding material to be learned so that we can perceive it from both the student's and the instructor's viewpoint.

Most students who are making average grades object to the idea of tutoring others because they feel that they do not know enough about the subject and might mislead rather than help. A great many of such students, however, have a higher degree of competence than they think they have. One reason their grades are not better is that they have hitherto lacked the opportunity to organize what they know. Tutoring, of course, will give them that opportunity. In any event, the proposal is one in which both participants have nothing to lose and may even gain something by giving it a try.

Using other students to improve motivation. I have said a great deal in this book about the desirability of using other people in the accomplishment of the tasks of learning and have perhaps given the impression that one should *only* study with others. If I have overstressed this approach, I should correct it here by saying that studying is essentially a lonely business. Most of the time that successful students spend on their work is spent alone. No one can write your papers, track down your references in the library, or read your books but you. It is the long hours that you spend with yourself and your books that will pay off in the end. All students know this. They may wish it were not true and they may try to find ways of shortcutting the process, but they know that the price that must be paid for success is measured in hundreds of hours of working alone.

If studying is essentially a lonely business, why then have I urged students to involve others in their study plans?

To answer this question, let us reexamine some of the basic facts about success in college. I have pointed out repeatedly that success is basically a matter of motivation. If an individual can pass college admission requirements, the chances are that he has the ability to succeed at least in some of the fields offered by the college. Certainly, some students are more competent and better prepared for college work than others, but there are successes and failures among students at *every* level of aptitude, from the highest to the lowest. A major difference (and very likely *the* major difference) between those who succeed at a given level of ability and those who fail is their motivation: their eagerness to succeed, their willingness to commit themselves to learning, and so on. The problem that plagues all students at some time or other is therefore a motivational one, one that may be expressed in these terms: "How can I generate and maintain interest in my work?" "How can I get myself to work when I don't want to?"

Some students are self-motivators. They can take themselves in hand and direct their attention toward matters that need work and involvement and away from interesting distractions. Most students, however, have difficulties in devoting themselves to their studies, particularly in courses that bore them or in which they resent the instructor. The problem is, essentially, that of enhancing motivation under unfavorable conditions. I have suggested a number of ways—getting to know the instructor, finding relationships between what is being taught and what one already knows, and the like—whereby students might be able to improve motivation on their own. These methods will work for some students and in some courses, but no approach works all the time, in all situations, and for all students. Something more is needed.

My suggestion that other people be used as a way of increasing motivation to learn is based on a considerable amount of psychological research that shows that many aspects of motivation are affected by our interaction with others. Working with others can, for example, raise interest in tasks·that otherwise may be dull and boring. We also take our cues from others. It is difficult to be with others and to carry on a working relationship with them without becoming involved in some of the activities that interest them. These are but two of the ways that interaction with others may raise our motivational level.

A brief description of a research study in which group interaction was used to raise the creativity of participants will illustrate the point. In this study, students were given six minutes to write interesting and/or humorous captions for a cartoon, working alone. Then they were assembled in small groups and asked to write captions for a second cartoon. The groups were in session for a ten-minute period, during which members were instructed to work as a group, to interact as much as possible, and to see how many interesting captions they could produce. During the third phase of the experiment, the students worked alone once more in writing captions for a third cartoon. Results showed that the captions produced during the third phase of the experiment were more creative than those produced during the first phase (Lindgren and Lindgren, 1965a, 1965b).

Previous research with this type of discussion technique showed that individuals are more creative working alone than they are within the context of a group. (This is somewhat analogous to saying that students can study more effectively alone than they can in a group.) *This* research study, however, suggests that the quality of work done alone can be enhanced if it is interspersed with group interaction.

Three things may occur as a result of group participation. First, the task may become more interesting. Working with a group is usually more stimulating and exciting than working alone, and some of this excitement transfers to the task on which the group is working. Second, an individual's attitudes toward a task are likely to be influenced by the attitudes displayed by others in the group. This is the group norm effect that I have mentioned, an effect that tends to carry over to subsequent individual activity. A hitherto reluctant worker, who finds himself in the midst of a task-oriented group that is working hard to achieve some goal, has difficulty in maintaining a position of noninvolvement. Third, the participant who has, shall we say, only one approach to a task learns other ways to deal with it. Other members of the group become models for him and he begins to imitate their behavior. Furthermore, his attempts to work on the problem are reinforced by other members of the group.

The point is that interacting with others from time to time facilitates and stimulates learning. Although learning is a highly personal process, it can be enhanced and improved by occasional or even frequent involvement with others. The proper kind of involvement may, indeed, supply the necessary ingredient that makes the difference between success or failure for many a student.

Disadvantages in studying with others. A basic reason why interaction with others can facilitate learning is that everyone is motivated by strong social needs—we all need the company of others at some time or other, and being with others can be a satisfying thing in and of itself. And therein lies a danger. Interaction with others works as a learning aid precisely because of the social needs that we all have, but its very attractiveness may also interfere with the work that every student has to do by himself. A small group of students in a chemistry class may decide to get together for a half hour to talk about questions that may come up in tomorrow's quiz. The half hour stretches out to an hour. One of the group raises the question of whether they should not end the session so each can go off by himself and work on the areas in which he is weak. The members decide instead that they are making good progress and that they should stay in session. Within a few minutes, however, one of the members has mentioned an attractive but irrelevant subject—say, a protest march that has been planned for the following week—and the group finally breaks up hours later without having given further attention to chemistry. The decision the group made at the end of the first hour, namely that they were making good progress and should stay in session, was really an excuse to remain within the comfortable social embrace of the group and to postpone the tedious, lonely task of working alone. We can find all manner of reasonable excuses to avoid working alone and to come together with others in some kind of a social arrangement. We can use others in order to raise our motivational level and enhance our learning only if we can also exercise the self-discipline needed to break off the interaction on schedule.

Social interaction can be a powerful aid to learning, but it can also be a potent master.

Learning to solve problems. There is one other aspect of working with other students that should be mentioned here. Much of the work that students do when they leave college and enter upon their careers involves working with other people in some kind of problem-solving activity. Indeed, the work in most professions consists of collaborating with other people at various levels in solving problems of mutual interest. Teachers, for example, not only work with pupils but also must collaborate with administrators, other teachers, and nonteaching staff. The collaboration undertaken by teachers is aimed at the solution of problems: how to stimulate learning, how to make out the reports that the administration needs, and how to get supplies. Similar comments can be made about any other profession.

The solution of these problems calls for the development and strengthening of various kinds of communication skills. We have already noted the opportunities that college students have to improve themselves in this respect. The ability to communicate, however, is only one aspect of the entire process of solving problems in social contexts. People in the professions also must be able to work with others in planning and scheduling, in anticipating the reactions and behavior of others both in and out of the group, and in arriving at decisions through compromise and negotiation. These are highly complex skills and they are not learned quickly and

117

easily. Very often, these students who are most successful in their academic specialties are the ones who are least skilled in using group methods to solve problems. The use of others to facilitate learning is essentially a group approach to the solving of problems that students face in common. Hence it is not unlike the kinds of problems that will be solved through collaboration when they become established in their professions and as citizens in their communities. The fact that every student will eventually become involved in group problem solving is thus still another reason to begin learning the skills of social interaction during the college years.

CHAPTER EIGHT

Failure and its remedies

UNDER what conditions can a B student be considered to be a failure?

SHOULD students who are undecided about a vocation force themselves to make a choice?

Is it the task of vocational counselors to choose occupations for students?

UNDER what circumstances should you make use of a psychological clinic?

CAN group counseling (or group therapy) *really* help students who are failing?

Is a student who drops a course a "quitter?"

Is there a study technique that "has everything?"

IN what way are students like employees?

WHAT are the *basic* requirements for success in college?

FAILURE, as we shall consider it in this chapter, consists of disappointments: not performing according to our hopes and expectations, or not meeting our *own* standards. Failure thus includes the obvious—receiving D's and F's and flunking out of school—but it also includes the C that Hope Felix got when she expected a B or better and the B that Sam Fitch received when he was sure that he was making an A. Failure is a disconfirmation of dreams and expectations; conversely, it can also be what we were afraid we were going to get all along.

No program of academic self-improvement can succeed unless we have reason to believe that we are potential successes and are willing to make some changes in our behavior, as well as in the way in which we look at ourselves and the world.

This book began with an exploration of who college students are and who they wish to become. These are fundamental questions in any discussion of success and failure. Until at least some of the main issues in self-identity are resolved, students are likely to drift, dealing only intermittently and ineffectively with problems of motivation that continually present themselves. Let us begin this discussion, therefore, with a consideration of steps that can be taken to resolve some of these basic questions of identity.

Vocational counseling. Vocational choice appears to be a reasonable place to start. Research shows that students who have selected a vocational objective are likely to do better in college than students who have not. There are a number of reasons why this difference appears. One is that most, but not all, students who have selected an occupation have a better idea of who they are or, at least, who they are going to be. In our culture, the individual's occupation is an important part of his self—who he is. This is one reason why people who are strangers ask one another what kind of work they do. By finding out what a person does, we are enabled to come to some fairly valid conclusions about him. An occupation not only tells us the individual's educational level but also something about his views on life, his interests, and the way he relates to the world. Having this information enables us to empathize with him and hence to interact with him more effectively For the individual himself, having an occupation means that there is a place for him in society, which in turn enables him to organize his time, to deal with others, and to plan for the future. In other words, having an occupation reduces a great deal of ambiguity and provides an individual with a feeling of security.

I mention this point about identity and security because most people regard occupations primarily as sources of income, overlooking their psychological and sociological significance. Perhaps people who are well established in their occupations can afford to overlook such implications, but college students who have not selected an occupation or who are committed only tentatively to a future career ought to be aware of the psychological meanings that are attached to the occupations they are considering. Many students arrive at what proves to be a satisfactory choice of a vocation by trial and error or because they have more than the usual amount of both self-understanding and occupational information, but a great many others have to try a number of different fields before they hit upon one that suits them, and some, of course, go through life as vocational misfits.

One factor that helps improve the chances of finding a satisfactory occupation is the fact that most students are adaptable and can learn. When Ron Harris signed up as a physics major, he was not sure whether this was the right field for him. He had both C's and B's in science courses, and he also had a fair amount of talent as a cellist. As he progressed through the courses specified for a degree in physics, however, he found himself becoming more interested in the field, and his grades began to improve. He still retained an interest in music, but gradually reduced the amount of time he devoted to it.

What Ron was doing was learning to become a physicist. To be sure, he was taking courses that would give him the knowledge and skill he would need in that profession, but over and above this he was also learning a set of attitudes, values, and interests that are more characteristic of physicists than they are of people in other professions. The point is that people select occupations because of a compatibility between their skills and interests and those demanded

121

by the profession, but the profession *also* selects, in the sense that it shapes the behavior of individuals who train for it and eliminates those who, for one reason or another, are unable to adjust to its demands.

A college education is a process of "becoming," as we noted in the initial chapter, and this includes becoming a person suited to the roles of an occupation.

The student who has made a decision about a career probably is more effective academically than others who have not done so because he is more likely to see the effect on his everyday life of the decisions he has made and to plan his life accordingly. Furthermore, the courses he takes are more likely to interest him because he can see how they fit into the larger scheme of things.

The fact that students who have made vocational choices do better in college does not mean that those who are undecided should immediately make a choice. Some are undecided because they feel they must explore a number of academic majors before finding a field that suits them. This is a reasonable way to go about matters, although it depends on how it is done. Unless a student has in mind two or three fields that he is actively investigating, merely trying first one major field and then another can be a time-consuming, expensive process. Many students, too, have not made a choice because they are too critical. They do not know what they want in the way of a career; they only know what they do *not* want.

Students in colleges that offer a vocational counseling service are particularly fortunate, because they can discuss problems of occupational choice with experts who understand students as individuals, who know both the requirements of occupations and what colleges offer in the way of preparation. Contrary to popular belief, psychological testing is not their chief function. Students often come to a counseling center asking to "take a test that will show me what I am fitted for." Counselors do administer and interpret tests, but such testing as is done is incidental to the counseling process. Many students also assume that counselors make decisions for students, whereas their function is largely that of helping students

122

understand their interests and aptitudes, strengths and weaknesses. They can also be a valuable source of information on the kind of activities that occupations entail. Counselors can also be of help in educational matters. They know, for example, what courses are the most helpful, where one can get help with reading problems, what instructors are good sources of information on occupational fields, and so on.

Students who do not have access to vocational counselors are at a disadvantage, but there are other ways of getting help with problems of vocational choice. In the chapter on relations with instructors I suggested that the need for information regarding a certain field of specialization may be a legitimate reason to approach an instructor. Thus the student not only secures useful information but is able to get to know and understand the instructor better. Librarians may also direct students to sources of valuable information on occupations. There are many pamphlets and books devoted to explaining the prerequisites, training, and work opportunities for a variety of occupations. Other sources of information include periodicals published by various professions, trade journals, and magazines devoted to occupational data. Students almost universally report that librarians are very helpful when it comes to locating relevant reading material, not only on specific occupations but also study aids of all types.

I should also mention the "study skills centers" and special courses that many colleges (particularly junior colleges) have set up to help students who are encountering academic difficulties. Some of these centers and courses use up-to-date techniques in programmed instruction to bring students up to par in reading, mathematical skills, language skills, and in fundamental subject matter in a relatively short period of time. Many a student has learned more mathematics in six weeks of programmed instruction than he has in his previous twelve years in school.

Help with emotional problems. The problems of motivation that I have mentioned as being crucial in college success are usually tied in with other kinds of problems—inability to develop satisfactory relations with others, chronic rebelliousness against authority,

123

fits of depression, and feelings of guilt and unworthiness—these are all focal areas of difficulty that can affect everything in a student's life, including his studies. Virtually all students are troubled by severe emotional problems at some time or other. Some are able to maintain satisfactory progress in spite of such problems, but many find they have to drop a course or two or even leave school for a while in order to cope with a difficult situation. Some, of course, become academic casualties, while still others hover between barely passing and failing, working far below their capacity for success.

Many colleges today provide psychological clinics or counseling services for students who are under temporary or chronic emotional stress. Even colleges that do not have these facilities have referral services whereby students who are in need of help can be directed to off-campus clinics, agencies, or psychotherapists in private practice. Deans of men, deans of women, or other officers in charge of personnel services often make such referrals or may themselves be able to provide emergency help at times. There has been a steady increase in the number of colleges that make some kind of provision for students with emotional problems—if only a referral service—partly because people are more willing to face the need for psychological help these days and partly for a very practical reason: a student who is failing costs a college more in time, trouble, and expense than any dozen students who are doing satisfactory work. It therefore makes sense for colleges to give the kind of help that will keep students from failing. I mention these points because students are often embarrassed at having to ask persons in the college administration for assistance with problems that they feel somehow they should have been able to manage themselves. The fact is that everyone needs to turn to others at some time or other for help with problems that have suddenly become overwhelming.[1]

[1] Participation in psychotherapy may have dramatic effects. In one study, only 10 percent of students who had been treated had failed and dropped out of college over a two-year period, whereas 60 percent of a comparable group who had not received treatment had failed (Paul, 1968).

124

Students do not, however, have to be troubled by severe academic problems to take advantage of such services. In recent years, a number of colleges have organized group counseling sessions for students who have various types of adjustment problems. Such groups may meet for weekly hour-and-a-half sessions for a school term under the direction of a counseling psychologist or some other type of student personnel worker. Sometimes a group of students with similar problems is able to persuade a member of the psychology department to serve as a leader for their group. Other individuals who work with such groups include members of social welfare departments, counseling departments, and college chaplains.

Virtually every college has some kind of service for the student who is having academic problems, although sometimes a student must ask around in order to find out what they are. It may take a number of inquiries, but eventually he will encounter someone, usually in the office of the dean of students, who will know what the resources of the college are and which one would be appropriate for him.

It is often a good idea to take advantage of more than one service. For example, a student who is having academic problems because he is a slow reader may be helped both by getting group counseling and by enrolling in a remedial reading course. Undertaking some kind of remedial activity is important, be it counseling, attendance at a reading clinic, employment of a tutor, or whatever, because such involvement enables the student to come to grips with his problem. As long as he is not involved in doing something about his difficulties, he is in danger of sinking into a morass of discouragement and depression. Most students who get into academic trouble are initially not as badly off as they think they are. What often happens is that they experience a number of setbacks in rapid sequence, say, about the sixth week of the term. Instead of dropping a course or two or taking some other steps to rectify the matter, they become overwhelmed by a sense of failure, stop making further efforts, stay away from classes, do not work on assignments, and adopt a "what's the use" attitude. Too often they postpone seeking help until it is too late. The advantage of early involvement in activity aimed at improving the situation is that it gives the student some degree of leverage on his problem. It reminds him that the problem *does* have a solution and that he can do something about it.

One of the chief contributions that clinical services can provide is that of helping students face a rather fundamental problem: fear of failure. As I have mentioned elsewhere, is it impossible to learn without experiencing some failure. We do not, for instance, always succeed the first time we try. If we do not try at all, however, we can never learn and will never succeed. Our experiences in grade school and high school tend to be marked by too intense a preoccupation with the horrors and the disgrace of failure to the point where there is a tendency to become panicky and disorganized when failure is a distinct possibility. What counselors and psychotherapists can do is to help students face the inevitability of some failure and to get them to consider ways of coping with it and learning from it whenever it occurs.

It is difficult for students who are encountering difficulties to know whether to drop a course. A series of below-passing grades may mean that the student should try a different major field, or it may indicate more fundamental deficiencies. Counselors can be very helpful in these situations in advising whether to change majors, drop a few courses, change colleges, hire a tutor, or drop out of college altogether.

Some students, of course, *should* drop out of college for a term or two at least, in order to reassess their goals and the resources they have with which to meet them. Moves like these that involve major changes in hopes and plans are naturally harder to plan than are minor decisions like dropping a course. They are often quite disturbing. The need to leave school is, however, often more traumatic and upsetting than it should be. The student who is dropping out is often ashamed to talk to counselors or instructors, feeling he has disgraced himself. Yet this type of failure can serve as an important opportunity for reassessment of goals. Furthermore, there may be ways whereby a readmission can be arranged after a period of time, and plans for remedial work during the interim can be discussed.

Signals of impending failure. People who eventually are dropped from enrollment in college because of failing grades— that is, who flunk out—almost always send out signals long before the actual event. The signals are clear and can be read by anyone who is looking for them. The signals that are most common are nonattendance, not completing assignments, and not taking quizzes and examinations. Unfortunately, other people, such as fellow students and instructors, are usually preoccupied with their own problems and the signals of distress usually go unnoticed. It is important that the signals also be received by the failing student, the person most concerned. Even though he is telling himself, in effect, that he is headed for disaster, he is as likely to ignore the signals as is anyone else. It is almost as though he *wants* to commit academic suicide.

Let me go over this again, because it is quite important. The student who misses more than one or two classes, or who fails to turn in assignments or to take quizzes, is telling the world, including himself, that he is headed for academic failure. These signs should be taken seriously and call for immediate action.

Dropping courses. What kind of action? For one thing, the student should see the instructor to find out where he stands. It may be possible to make up the missed work without penalty. If this is possible, the student should ask himself seriously whether his attitude toward the course has changed enough to enable him to invest the amount of time and energy required. Make-up work also has to be fitted in with regular assignments in the same course and in other courses. This is an added burden; the student should be honest with himself and not overly optimistic.

The student should also seriously consider whether he should drop the course officially. Many students regard dropping a course as weak-kneed or even cowardly, and some instructors tacitly encourage this attitude by encouraging students who should never have taken the course to stay on until the end. Most colleges, however, have a "W" (withdrawal type of grade) for those who drop out of a course before the end of a term, provided they were doing passing work up to that point. The W grade is neutral; it counts neither for nor against the student. Students drop courses for all kinds of reasons, and a W grade is no disgrace.

There are many advantages in dropping a course in which you have made a bad start. It may well be that there is some degree of incompatibility between you and the instructor. It is too much to expect that you should be able to learn equally well from all instructors, and it seems the better part of wisdom to drop a course taught by an incompatible instructor and to sign up for the same course with a different instructor the following term. Some students follow the practice of "shopping around" during the first week of the term while course changes can be made without penalty. This enables them to get courses with more compatible instructors and to avoid courses with those who are less compatible. A disadvantage to this method is that one or two class sessions may not be a fair sample of an instructor's style, and communication problems may develop later in the term that were not anticipated during the first week. Another disadvantage is that the student who picks only obviously compatible instructors may be selecting learning situations that are too "sheltered"—that is, unless he exposes himself to a variety of instructional styles, he may be missing some important opportunities to learn and to grow intellectually. Students who select their instructors by this method create problems for the college registrar, who should not then be criticized if the other services he provides (such as the reporting of grades and the issuing of transcripts) are slowed down as a result of the change-of-course workload. This is not to say that students should not consider such factors as compatibility when they select an instructor, but it is to say that they should realize what they are doing when they "shop around."

To return to the problem of the student who realizes that he is beginning to fail in a course, the best decision for him to make may be that of dropping the course and taking a "W." This move will not only get him out of a difficult situation but it will give him more time to devote to other subjects. If he has already fallen below the passing level, and the instructor insists that he take an "FW" (withdrawal under failing conditions) for dropping the course, more heroic measures are obviously indicated. I have suggested a number of them: hiring a tutor, seeking help from counselors or clinics, revising strategies or developing new ones.

A study technique that "has everything." I have made two points repeatedly: (1) learning is a personal matter: no one can learn for us, just as no one can grow or develop for us; and (2) the process of growth and development that we term learning can be facilitated and enhanced if we make intelligent use of other people. I have also pointed out that these two principles are not contradictory. Indeed, they may be used to complement each other. The major problem in learning seems to be that of devising strategies that ensure the kind of involvement and activity that will lead to intellectual growth and that will at the same time make some appropriate use of others. Such strategies are likely to be more successful when the other individuals also receive benefits from helping us.

Now I shall describe a technique or strategy that combines both of these features. I do not suggest it as a method that "everyone should use" because there is probably no method that will work for everyone. Also the method has some special conditions that must be met if it is to be really helpful. Moreover, it has the disadvantage of being appropriate primarily in courses for which there is an assigned textbook, or textbooks, in which much of the class time is spent in lecture, and in which there are a number of quizzes or examinations during the term. Courses that are built around student participation will naturally call for other types of strategies.

Finally, I present this strategy or technique primarily as an example or model that combines the features we have noted as desirable for a satisfactory learning experience: it involves you in an activity designed to promote learning and it brings you into contact with others who are in a position to help you. If carried out properly, it can make studying a stimulating and interesting experience; it makes it more of a game and less of a steady, dreary slogging through endless reaches of printed page. It is also a method that has been used with considerable success both by students who were interested in getting the most out of a course (and, incidentally, making top grades) and by those who have fallen behind and want to catch up and reestablish themselves.

The student who wishes to try the proposed method must satisfy these preconditions: he must have a partner who is willing to work with him and to use the same method; he and his partner must be willing to try an experimental approach; and there must be a quiz or an examination in the offing that will provide an opportunity to try out the experiment.

The method calls for you and your partner to work separately, each preparing a true-false test consisting of one question for each page of that portion of the textbook which is to be covered by the examination. The questions do not have to be elegantly phrased, but they should deal with some significant fact or concept, and not with trivialities. Competing to see who can come up with the most ingenious questions will add to the interest of the experiment. Writing "trick questions" to catch the partner unawares is perfectly legitimate—it is only a game, and even those who lose will win when examination day comes. The one-question-per-page requirement is flexible. If there are four hundred pages to be covered, the number of questions can be reduced to one every two pages or so. If the amount of material to be covered is brief and contains many facts and concepts, one question per page may be insufficient. Both partners must write questions on the same material. Six hundred pages of text should not be divided up in terms of three hundred pages for each partner. The purpose of the strategy is that of promoting *learning through involvement,* not that of saving time and energy. Your primary gain results from the questions *you* write; answering your partner's questions later is a *necessary* step in the process, but it is of *secondary* importance.

Lecture notes can also provide material for true-false questions, but you have to be the judge in this instance of how intensively it is to be covered.

Then you and your partner should set aside a period or periods of two to three hours, preferably a day or so before the scheduled examination, as a time to come together and test each other orally on the questions. It does not matter what procedure you follow when you get together with your partner, but the general idea is that each member of the pair poses his questions, one by one, and the other member tries to answer them.

Let us now review the procedure and try to determine why students have found it to be successful.

If you read over material in search of ideas on which to base a true-false question, you will look at it in a different way than if you are only trying to absorb facts. Reading for absorption is likely to be passive; looking for concepts and information that can be used to frame questions is active. The method therefore is more likely to *involve* you more than merely reading for retention.

One of the problems in studying a textbook is attention. We have all had the experience of reading a page or two and then realizing that we cannot remember a thing we have read. This may happen under any type of condition, but particularly when we are tired, when the material is especially abstruse, or when we dislike the course or the book. The question-writing plan has the advantage of adding an element of interest: it gives us something to do other than merely passively covering the material.

A third advantage is that when you use the technique, you are forced to play the role of the evaluator—you must look at the material with the eye of an individual preparing a test. This is a role that students seldom assume and, as I pointed out in the chapter on communication, if you are able to approach material to be learned from the point of view of the instructor (or anyone else who writes test items), you have a distinct advantage over students who have an essentially one-dimensional approach to studying. Incidentally, it does not matter what type of question the instructor will use in the examination to come. The proposed strategy works best if the test is to be objective—multiple-choice, true-false, matching, short-answer, or whatever—but students have reported that they found the method also helpful in preparing for essay examinations. If the scheduled examination is to be entirely essay, however, it may be well to include some essay questions for each chapter or lecture to be covered.

The reasons I have given for writing true-false questions would hold true, of course, even if you worked alone and did not have a partner with whom you planned to meet shortly before the examination. You could, therefore, dispense with the partner and work entirely alone. The session with the partner, however, does provide some extra advantages. It gives you a deadline by which you must have your questions ready. Without such a deadline, it is very easy to slip back into the more passive approach—that of merely reading the textbook—that most students use.

A second and more significant advantage derives from the interaction that takes place between the partners. The fact that the questions you will write are actually going to be used to test someone makes them more important, and you will be inclined to give them more careful attention. Some of the questions and answers will inevitably be challenged, and there is usually a great deal of checking back with the book to ascertain the correct answer. This is all to the good and opens up fresh viewpoints. Misconceptions and misinterpretations of the text are thus cleared up. Furthermore, a little controversy always makes things more interesting and adds to the excitement of the game.

Still another advantage to the interaction is that of being exposed to the other person's questions. Any two individuals will predictably develop different understandings of the same material, and trying to answer another person's questions leads to an awareness of points of view other than your own.

Finally, this second phase of this experimental method gives you an opportunity to interact with another individual with whom you can share a problem and its solution. Getting together with a partner on a mutually beneficial enterprise enables you to satisfy some of the social needs that every person has and must meet.

The technique, as I have described it, sounds very simple, but many students have difficulty in carrying it through. The chief problem is that of finding another student who is willing to fulfill his part of the bargain and write his questions. If it is impossible to find such a person, something may still be salvaged by finding an individual who is willing to *answer* questions. This should be relatively easy, because there are many students who are happy to review for a test if someone else will make the arrangements and do most of the work. The person who writes the test items nevertheless gets the best of such a bargain, because he is the one who has the advantage of reading the text in a different way.

Another problem arises from students' unwillingness to spend time on writing questions while reviewing the text. The task takes extra time and concentration, and students who are really not very committed to the idea of studying will naturally find ways of begging off. The technique is only for those who are willing to take the psychological risk of involving themselves in an active (as contrasted with a passive) learning experience.

ACADEMIC SUCCESS AS A ROUTINE

The method I just described is most effective in preparing for examinations, although it has features that can be adapted to other types of studying. For instance, there is no reason why students who are reading a textbook for the first time cannot write true-false items as they go along and save them for a later, preexamination review, alone or with other students. I have presented the method here, however, because it is an interesting kind of game which, if properly played, can have a dramatic effect on examination grades. If conducted according to the rules I have specified, it can be used to pull a failing student back onto safe ground or move a "B" student into "A" territory. The technique is, nevertheless, a form of "treatment" rather than a regimen that can be followed over a long period of time.

What will work in the long run to keep students from failing and to provide a firm basis for academic success is the development of a routine—a day-by-day or week-by-week approach to learning that will enable them to have a reasonable amount of success under most conditions.

Before I discuss the routine in detail, let me make some observations about the student's role in college, some observations that may be obvious, but that point up a relationship that is often overlooked.

Your role as a student is not unlike that of an employee. You are given certain tasks or assignments to perform and you are paid in terms of credits: units completed and grades or marks. The college may, in this sense, be regarded as the corporation in which you are employed, and in which the instructors play the role of employment supervisors. Like corporations, colleges formulate general policies and programs of work to be accomplished. Instructors are, however, given a great deal more latitude than supervisors usually receive in determining how much work should be performed and what standards shall be used in evaluation.

To carry this analogy somewhat further, students are like employees paid on an incentive plan, who are expected to maintain certain minimum standards of quality in production and are given extra rewards for exceeding these minimums. In order to remain employed and to earn at least the minimum wage, employees, among other things, are supposed to come to work on time, to be absent only because of illness or some other emergency, and to complete work within specified time limits. To receive higher levels of reward, they must still conform to the minimum standards I have described.

Students, too, are expected to conform to the minimum standards specified by the college and by their instructors if they are to receive passing grades, and the awarding of higher grades also assumes that the minimum standards are met. The minimum standards are so obvious that they are known to every student: regular and prompt attendance at classes, completion of assignments when due, reading assigned books, and taking of quizzes and examinations whenever they are scheduled.

All this may seem so self-evident that it is not worth mentioning. Nevertheless, most students who fail have not met these minimum requirements. In the survey of successful and unsuccessful students at San Francisco State College, mentioned in Chapter Three, less than 10 percent of the successful students had poor attendance, as contrasted with almost 40 percent of the unsuccessful ones. Significantly, more of the successful students met deadlines for papers as well. We are not concerned here with the reasons *why* unsuccessful students do not have better attendance and do not meet deadlines; I have discussed this topic a number of times at various points in the book. Nor are we concerned with the fact that some highly successful students have poor class attendance and miss deadlines for assignments. By any standard, such students are unusual in the sense that they are able to convince their instructors that they deserve special consideration for one reason or another. These are students who have something extra to offer and who have some solid base from which they can negotiate with their instructors. To use the employment analogy, the nonconforming, bright students are like star salesmen who enjoy special privileges because of their high productivity. Average students or average employees do not have this "extra something" to offer; hence they are flirting with danger if they try to shape the rules to suit themselves.

The major differences in the behavior displayed by the great majorities of successful students and failing students show that the most dependable way of avoiding failure in college is to do what is required of one. This principle works in college, just as it does in employment situations. The students who have the best chances for success are those who have set up a routine whereby it is almost second nature to show up for class, to complete assignments on time, and to take examinations as required. This may not be a very original or exciting way to succeed, nor does it provide any short cuts. It does require self-discipline, planning, scheduling, and the investment of much time and energy.

In the end, however, it all comes back to the question of motivation. Students who are motivated to succeed and who are willing to let the college experience change them are the ones who develop the kind of routine that enables them to meet at least the minimum demands of their instructors. If they are successful in solving the problem of motivation, however, they are also likely to go beyond these minimum demands and to involve themselves deeply in the learning processes. For such students, attending college is more than a routine exercise—it is an opportunity to *become*.

REFERENCES

Bruner, J. S., Goodnow, J. J., and Austin, G. A., *A study of thinking.* New York: Wiley, 1956.

Combs, Arthur W., and Snygg, Donald, *Individual behavior,* rev. ed. New York: Harper, 1959.

Drucker, Peter F., How to be an employee, *Fortune,* 1952, **45** (May), 126-127.

Gage, N. L., Runkel, P. J., and Chatterjee, B. B., *Equilibrium theory and behavior change: an experiment in feed back from pupils to teachers.* Urbana, Ill.: Bureau of Educational Research, University of Illinois, 1960.

Gough, Harrison G., *Manual for the California Psychological Inventory.* Palo Alto, Calif.: Consulting Psychologists Press, 1957.

Heilbrun, Alfred B., Jr., Personality factors in college dropout. *Journal of Applied Psychology,* 1965, **49,** 1-7.

Holland, John L., The prediction of college grades from the California Psychological Inventory and the Scholastic Aptitude Test, *Journal of Educational Psychology,* 1959, **50,** 135-142.

Kitzhaber, Albert R., *Themes, theories and therapy: the teaching of writing in college.* New York: McGraw-Hill, 1963.

Lindgren, H. C., and Lindgren, F., Brainstorming and orneriness as facilitators of creativity, *Psychological Reports,* 1965, **16,** 577-583. (a)

Lindgren, H. C., and Lindgren, F., Creativity, brainstorming, and orneriness: a cross-cultural study, *Journal of Social Psychology,* 1965, **67,** 23-30. (b)

Marks, E., Student perceptions of college persistence, and their intellective, personality, and performance correlates, *Journal of Educational Psychology,* 1967, **58,** 210-221.

Maslow, A. H., *Toward a psychology of being*. Princeton: Van Nostrand, 1962.

Paul, G. L., Two year follow-up of systematic desensitization in therapy groups, *Journal of Abnormal Psychology*, 1968, **73**, 119-130.

Riesman, D., Student culture and faculty values. In Margaret L. Habein, editor, *Spotlight on the college student*. Washington: American Council on Education, 1959.

Rogers, C. R., *On becoming a person*. Boston: Houghton Mifflin, 1961.

Trent, J. W., and Medsker, L. L., *Beyond high school*. San Francisco: Jossey-Bass, 1968.

Index